FOOLED
BY
RANDOMNESS

About the author

Nassim Nicholas Taleb is the founder of Empirica Capital LLC, a crisis-hunting hedge fund operator, and a fellow at the Courant Institute of Mathematical Sciences of New York University. He has held a variety of derivative trading positions in New York and London and worked as an independent floor trader in Chicago. Taleb was inducted in February 2001 in the *Derivatives Strategy* Hall of Fame.

Taleb received an MBA from the Wharton School and a Ph.D. from University Paris-Dauphine. He is the author of *Dynamic Hedging: Managing Vanilla and Exotic Options* (Wiley, 1997).

FOOLED
BY
RANDOMNESS

The Hidden Role of Chance
in the Markets and in Life

NASSIM NICHOLAS TALEB

TEXERE

New York • London

Published in 2001 by

TEXERE LLC
55 East 52nd Street
New York, NY 10055

Tel: +1 (212) 317 5511
Fax: +1 (212) 317 5178
www.etexere.com

UK subsidiary office

TEXERE Publishing Limited
71–77 Leadenhall Street
London EC3A 3DE

Tel: +44 (0)20 7204 3644
Fax: +44 (0)20 7208 6701
www.etexere.co.uk

This publication is designed to provide accurate and authoritative information in
regard to the subject matter covered. It is sold with the understanding that the
publisher is not engaged in rendering legal, accounting, or other professional services.
If legal advice or other expert assistance is required, the services of a competent
professional person should be sought.

Designed by The Book Design Group

Project managed by Macfarlane Production Services, Markyate, Hertfordshire,
England (e-mail: macfarl@aol.com)
Typeset by MHL Typesetting Ltd, Coventry, Warwickshire, England

Library of Congress Cataloging-in-Publication Data has been applied for.

ISBN 1-58799-071-7

Printed in the United States of America

This book is printed on acid-free paper.

To my mother

Minerva Ghosn Taleb

CONTENTS

✛

PREFACE AND ACKNOWLEDGMENTS

This book is the synthesis of, on one hand, the no-nonsense mathematical trader (self-styled "practitioner of uncertainty") who spent his life trying to resist being fooled by randomness and trick the emotions associated with uncertainty and, on the other, the aesthetically obsessed, literature-loving human being willing to be fooled by any form of nonsense that is polished, refined, original, and tasteful. I am not capable of avoiding being the fool of randomness; what I can do is confine it to where it brings some aesthetic gratification.

Much has been written about our biases (acquired or genetic) in dealing with randomness over the past decade. My rules while writing this book have been to avoid discussing (a) anything that I did not either personally witness on the topic or develop independently, and (b) anything that I have not distilled well enough to be able to write on the subject with the slightest effort. Everything that remotely felt like work was out. I had to purge the text from passages that seemed to come from a visit to the library, including the scientific name dropping. I tried to use no quote that does not naturally spring from my memory and does not come from a writer whom I have intimately frequented over the years (I detest the practice of random use of borrowed wisdom – much on that, later). *Aut tace aut loquere meliora silencio* (only when the words outperform silence).

I tried to make the minimum out of my direct profession of mathematical trader. Markets are a mere special case of randomness traps. I discuss them in an illustrative way as I would in a dinner conversation with, say, a cardiologist with intellectual curiosity (I used as a model my second-generation friend Jacques Merab).

Some acknowledgments: first, I would like to thank friends who can be considered rightful co-authors. I am grateful to New York intellectual and expert in randomness Stan Jonas (I do not know any other designation that would do him justice) for half a lifetime of conversations into all subjects bordering on probability with the animation and the zeal of the neophyte. I thank my probabilist friend Don Geman (husband of Helyette Geman, my thesis director) for his enthusiastic support for my book; he also made me realize that probabilists are born, not made – many mathematicians are capable of computing, but not understanding, probability (they are no better than the general population in exerting probabilistic judgments). The real book started with an all-night conversation with my erudite friend Jamil Baz during the summer of 1987, as he discussed the formation of "new" and "old" money among families. I was then a budding trader and he scorned the arrogant Salomon Brothers traders that surrounded him (he was proved right). He instilled in me the voracious introspection about my performance in life and really gave me the idea for this book. Both of us ended up getting doctorates later in life, on an almost identical subject matter. I have also dragged many people on (very long) walks in New York, London, or Paris, discussing some parts of this book, such as the late Jimmy Powers, who helped nurture my trading early on, and who kept repeating "anyone can buy and sell", or my encyclopedic friend David Pastel equally at ease with literature, mathematics, and Semitic languages. I have also engaged my lucid Popperian colleague Jonathan Waxman in numerous conversations on the integration of Karl Popper's ideas in our life as traders.

Second, I have been lucky to meet Myles Thompson and David Wilson, when they both were at J. Wiley & Sons. Myles has vision – he is the reverse "me too" publisher. He understands that books need not be written to satisfy a pre-defined labeled audience, but that a book will find its own unique set of readers – thus giving more credit to the reader than the off-the-rack publisher. As to David, he believed enough in the book to push me to take it into its natural course, free of all labels and taxonomies. David saw me the way I view myself; someone who has a passion for probability and randomness, who is obsessed with literature but happens to be a trader, rather than a generic "expert". He also saved my idiosyncratic style from the dulling of the editing process (for all its faults, the style is *mine*). Finally, Mina Samuels proved to be the greatest conceivable editor: immensely intuitive, cultured, aesthetically concerned, yet nonintrusive.

Many friends have fed me with ideas during conversations, ideas that found their way into the text. I can mention the usual suspects, all of them prime conversationalists: Cynthia Shelton Taleb, Helyette Geman, Marie-Christine Riachi, Paul Wilmott, Shaiy Pilpel, David DeRosa, Eric Briys, Sid Kahn, Jim Gatheral, Bernard Oppetit, Cyrus Pirasteh, Martin Mayer, Bruno Dupire, Raphael Douady, Marco Avellaneda, Didier Javice, Neil Chriss, and Philippe Asseily.

Some of these chapters were composed and discussed as part of the "Odeon Circle", as my friends and I met with a varying degree of regularity (on Wednesdays at 10 p.m. after my Courant class) at the bar of the restaurant Odeon in Tribecca. *Genius loci* ("the spirit of the place") and outstanding Odeon staff member Tarek Khelifi made sure that we were well taken care of and enforced our assiduity by making me feel guilty on no-shows, thus helping greatly with the elaboration of the book. We owe him a lot.

I must also acknowledge the people who read the MS, diligently helped with the errors, or contributed to the elaboration of the book with useful comments: Inge Ivchenko, Danny Tosto, Manos Vourkoutiotis, Stan Metelits, Jack Rabinowitz, Silverio Foresi, Achilles Venetoulias, and Nicholas Stephanou. Erik Stettler was invaluable in his role as a shadow copy editor. All mistakes are mine.

Finally, many versions of this book sat on the web, yielding sporadic (and random) bursts of letters of encouragement, corrections, and valuable questions which made me weave answers into the text. Many chapters of this book came in response to readers' questions. Francesco Corielli from Bocconi alerted me on the biases in the dissemination of scientific results.

This book was written and finished after I founded Empirica, my intellectual home, "Camp Empirica", in the woods in the back country of Greenwich, CT, which I designed to fit my taste and feel like a hobby; a combination of an applied probability research laboratory, athletic summer camp, and, not least, a crisis hunting hedge fund operation (I had experienced one of my best professional years while writing these lines). I thank all the like-minded people who helped fuel the stimulating atmosphere there: Pallop Angsupun, Danny Tosto, Peter Halle, Mark Spitznagel, Yuzhang Zhou, and Cyril de Lambilly as well as the members of Paloma Partners such as Tom Witz who challenged our wisdom on a daily basis or Donald Sussman who supplied me with his penetrating judgment.

CHAPTER SUMMARIES

One: If You're So Rich Why Aren't You So Smart?

An illustration of the effect of randomness on social pecking order and jealousy, through two characters of opposite attitudes. On the concealed rare event. How things in modern life may change rather rapidly, except, perhaps, in dentistry.

Two: A Bizarre Accounting Method

On alternative histories, a probabilistic view of the world, intellectual fraud, and the randomness wisdom of a Frenchman with steady bathing habits. How journalists are bred to not understand random series of events. Beware borrowed wisdom: how almost all great ideas concerning random outcomes are against conventional sapience. On the difference between correctness and intelligibility.

Three: A Mathematical Meditation on History

On Monte Carlo simulation as a metaphor to understanding a sequence of random historical events. On randomness and artificial history. Age is beauty, almost always, and the new and the young are generally toxic. Send your history professor to an introductory class on sampling theory.

Four: Randomness, Nonsense, and the Scientific Intellectual

On extending the Monte Carlo generator to produce artificial thinking and compare it with rigorous non-random constructs. The science wars enter the business world. Why the aesthete in me loves to be fooled by randomness.

Five: Survival of the Least Fit – Can Evolution Be Fooled by Randomness?

A case study on two rare events. On rare events and evolution. How "Darwinism" and evolution are concepts that are misunderstood in the non-biological world. Life is not continuous. How evolution will be fooled by randomness. A preparation to the problem of induction.

Six: Skewness and Asymmetry

We introduce the concept of skewness: why the terms "bull" and "bear" have limited meaning outside of zoology. A vicious child wrecks the structure of randomness. An introduction to the problem of epistemological opacity. The penultimate step before the problem of induction.

Seven: The Problem of Induction

On the chromodynamics of swans. Taking Solon's warning into some philosophical territory. How Victor Niederhoffer taught me empiricism; I added deduction. Why it is not scientific to take science seriously. Soros promotes Popper. That bookstore on 21st and Fifth Avenue. Pascal's wager.

Eight: Too Many Millionaires Next Door

Three illustrations of the survivorship bias. Why very few people should live on Park Avenue. The millionaire next door has very flimsy clothes. An overcrowding of experts.

Nine: It Is Easier To Buy and Sell Than Fry an Egg

Some technical extensions of the survivorship bias. On the distribution of "coincidences" in life. It is preferable to be lucky than competent (but you can be caught). The birthday paradox. More charlatans (and more journalists). How the researcher with work ethics can find just about anything in data. On dogs not barking.

Ten: Loser Takes All – On the Nonlinearities of Life

The nonlinear viciousness of life. Moving to Bel Air and acquiring the vices of the rich and famous. Why Microsoft's Bill Gates may not be the best in his business (but please do not inform him of such a fact). Depriving donkeys of food.

Eleven: Randomness and Our Brain: We Are Probability Blind

On the difficulty of thinking of your vacation as a linear combination of Paris and the Bahamas. Nero Tulip may never ski in the Alps again. Some discussion of behavioral discoveries. Some manifestations of probability blindness taken out of a textbook. A little more on journalistic pollution. Why you may be dead by now.

Twelve: Gamblers' Ticks and Pigeons in a Box

On gamblers' ticks crowding up my life. Why bad taxi-cab English can help you make money. How I am the fool of all fools, except that I am aware of it. Dealing with my genetic unfitness. No boxes of chocolate under my trading desk.

Thirteen: Carneades Comes to Rome: On Probability and Skepticism

Cato the censor sends Carneades packing. Monsieur de Norpois does not remember his old opinions. Beware the scientist. Marrying ideas. The same Robert Merton helping the author start his firm. Science evolves from funeral to funeral.

Fourteen: Bacchus Abandons Antony

Montherlant's death. Stoicism is not the stiff upper lip, but the illusion of victory of man against randomness. It is so easy to be heroic. Randomness and personal elegance.

PROLOGUE

Mosques in the Clouds

This book is about luck disguised and perceived as non-luck (that is, skills) and, more generally, randomness disguised and perceived as non-randomness (that is, determinism). It manifests itself in the shape of the *lucky fool*, defined as a person who benefited from a disproportionate share of luck but attributes his success to some other, generally very precise, reason. Such confusion crops up in the most unexpected areas, even science, though not in such an accentuated and obvious manner as it does in the world of business. It is endemic in politics, as it can be encountered in the shape of a country's president discoursing on the jobs that "he" created, "his" recovery, and "his predecessor's" inflation.

We are genetically still very close to our ancestors who roamed the savannah. The formation of our beliefs is fraught with superstitions – even today (I might say, especially today). Just as one day some primitive tribesman scratched his nose, saw rain falling, and developed an elaborate method of scratching his nose to bring on the much-needed rain, we link economic prosperity to some rate cut by the Federal Reserve Board, or the success of a company with the appointment of the new president "at the helm". Bookstores are full of biographies of successful men and women presenting their specific explanation on how they made it big in life (we have an expression, "the right time and the right place" to weaken whatever conclusion can be inferred from them).

This confusion strikes people of different persuasions; the literature professor invests a deep meaning into a mere coincidental occurrence of word patterns, while the financial statistician proudly detects "regularities" and "anomalies" in data that are plain random.

At the cost of appearing biased, I have to say that the literary mind can be intentionally prone to the confusion between *noise* and *meaning*, that is, between a randomly constructed arrangement and a precisely intended message. However, this causes little harm; few claim that art is a tool of investigation of the Truth – rather than an attempt to escape it or make it more palatable. Symbolism is the child of our inability and unwillingness to accept randomness; we give meaning to all manner of shapes; we detect human figures in inkblots. *I saw mosques in the clouds* announced Arthur Rimbaud the 19th-century French symbolic poet. This interpretation took him to "poetic" Abyssinia (in East Africa), where he was brutalized by a Christian Lebanese slave dealer, contracted syphilis, and lost a leg to gangrene. He gave up poetry in disgust at the age of 19, and died anonymously in a Marseilles hospital ward while still in his thirties. But it was too late. European intellectual life developed what seems to be an irreversible taste for symbolism – we are still paying its price, with psychoanalysis and other fads.

Regrettably, some people play the game too seriously; they are paid to read too much into things. All my life I have suffered the conflict between my love of literature and poetry and my profound allergy to most teachers of literature and "critics". The French poet Paul Valery was surprised to listen to a commentary of his poems that found meanings that had until then escaped him (of course, it was pointed out to him that these were intended by his subconscious).

More generally, we underestimate the share of randomness in about anything, a point that may not merit a book – except when it is the specialist who is the fool of all fools. Disturbingly, science has only recently been able to handle randomness (the growth in available information has been exceeded by the expansion of noise). Probability theory is a young arrival in mathematics; probability applied to practice is almost nonexistent as a discipline.

Consider the left and the right columns of Table P.1. The best way to summarize the major thesis of this book is that it addresses situations (many of them tragicomical) where the left column is mistaken for the

Table P.1 Table of Confusion
Presenting the central distinctions used in the book

GENERAL

Luck	Skills
Randomness	Determinism
Probability	Certainty
Belief, conjecture	Knowledge, certitude
Theory	Reality
Anecdote, coincidence	Causality, law
Forecast	Prophecy

MARKET PERFORMANCE

Lucky idiot	Skilled investor
Survivorship bias	Market outperformance

FINANCE

Volatility	Return (or drift)
Stochastic variable	Deterministic variable

PHYSICS AND ENGINEERING

Noise	Signal

LITERARY CRITICISM

None (literary critics do not seem to have a name for things they do not understand)	Symbol

PHILOSOPHY OF SCIENCE

Epistemic probability	Physical probability
Induction	Deduction
Synthetic proposition	Analytic proposition

right one. The sub-sections also illustrate the key areas of discussion on which this book will be based.

The reader may wonder whether the opposite case might not deserve some attention, that is, the situations where non-randomness is mistaken for randomness. Shouldn't we be concerned with situations where patterns and messages may have been ignored? I have two answers. First, I am not overly worried about the existence of undetected patterns. We have been reading lengthy and complex messages in just about any manifestation of nature that presents jaggedness (such as the palm of a hand, the residues at the bottom of Turkish coffee cups, etc.). Armed with home supercomputers and chained processors, and helped by complexity and "chaos" theories, the scientists, semi-scientists, and pseudoscientists will be able to find portents. Second, we need to take into account the costs of mistakes; in my opinion, mistaking the right column for the left one is not as costly as an error in the opposite direction. Even popular opinion warns that bad information is worse than no information at all.

However interesting these areas could be, their discussion would be a tall order. In addition, they are not my current professional specialty. There is one world in which I believe the habit of mistaking luck for skill is most prevalent – and most conspicuous – and that is the world of trading. By luck or misfortune, that is the world in which I operate. It is my profession, and as such it will form the backbone of this book. It is what I know best. In addition, business presents the best (and most entertaining) laboratory for the understanding of these differences. For it is the area of human undertaking where the confusion is greatest and its effects the most pernicious. For instance, we often have the mistaken impression that a strategy is an excellent strategy, or an entrepreneur a person endowed with "vision", or a trader an excellent trader, only to realize that 99.9% of their past performance is attributable to chance, and chance alone. Ask a profitable investor to explain the reasons for his success; he will offer some deep and convincing interpretation of the results. Frequently, these delusions are intentional and deserve to bear the name "charlatanism".

If there is one cause for this confusion between the left and the right sides of our table, it is our inability to think critically – we may enjoy presenting conjectures as truth. We are wired to be like that. We will see that our mind is not equipped with the adequate hardware to handle probabilities; such infirmity even strikes the expert, sometimes just the expert. A critical mind, on the other hand, is someone who has the guts, when confronting a given set of information, to attribute a large share of its possible cause to the left column.

The 19th-century cartoon character, pot-bellied bourgeois Monsieur Prudhomme, carried around a large sword with a double intent:

primarily to defend the Republic against its enemies, and secondarily to attack it should it stray from its course. In the same manner, this book has two purposes: to defend science (as a light beam across the noise of randomness), and to attack the scientist when he strays from his course (most disasters come from the fact that individual scientists do not have an innate understanding of standard error or a clue about critical thinking). As a practitioner of uncertainty I have seen more than my share of snake-oil salesmen dressed in the garb of scientists. The greatest fools of randomness will be found among these.

This author hates books that can be easily guessed from the table of contents – but a hint of what comes next seems in order. The book is composed of three parts. The first is an introspection into Solon's warning, as his outburst on rare events became my lifelong motto. In it we meditate on visible and invisible histories. The second presents a collection of probability biases I encountered (and suffered from) in my career in randomness – ones that continue to fool me. The third concludes the book with the revelation that perhaps ridding ourselves of our humanity is not in the works; we need tricks, not some grandiose moralizing help. Again the elders can help us with some of their ruses.

PART I

SOLON'S WARNING - SKEWNESS, ASYMMETRY, INDUCTION

Croesus, King of Lydia, was considered the richest man of his time. To this day Romance languages use the expression "rich as Croesus" to describe a person of excessive wealth. He was said to be visited by Solon, the Greek legislator known for his dignity, reserve, upright morals, humility, frugality, wisdom, intelligence, and courage. Solon did not display the smallest surprise at the wealth and splendor surrounding his host, nor the tiniest admiration for their owner. Croesus was so irked by the manifest lack of impression on the part of this illustrious visitor that he attempted to extract from him some acknowledgment. He asked him if he had known a happier man than him. Solon cited the life of a man who led a noble life and died while in battle. Prodded for more, he gave similar examples of heroic but terminated lives, until Croesus, irate, asked him point-blank if he was not to be considered the happiest man of all. Solon answered: "The observation of the numerous misfortunes that attend all conditions forbids us to grow insolent upon our present enjoyments, or to admire a man's happiness that may yet, in course of time, suffer change. For the uncertain future has yet to come, with all variety of future; and him only to whom the divinity has [guaranteed] continued happiness until the end we may call happy."[1]

The modern equivalent has been no less eloquently voiced by the baseball coach Yogi Berra, who seems to have translated Solon's outburst from the pure Attic Greek into no less pure Brooklyn English with "it ain't over until it's over", or, in a less dignified manner, with "it ain't over until the fat lady sings". In addition, aside from his use of the vernacular, the Yogi Berra quote presents an advantage of being true, while the meeting between Croesus and Solon was one of these historical facts that benefited from the imagination of the chroniclers, as it was chronologically impossible for the two men to have been in the same location.

Part I is concerned with the degree to which a situation may yet, in the course of time, suffer change. For we can be tricked by situations involving mostly the activities of the Goddess Fortuna – Jupiter's firstborn daughter. Solon was wise enough to get the following point; that which came with the help of luck could be taken away by luck (and often rapidly and unexpectedly at that). The flipside, which deserves to be considered as well (in fact it is even more of our concern), is that things that come with little help from luck are more resistant to randomness. Solon also had the intuition of a problem that has obsessed science for the past three centuries. It is called the problem of induction. I call it in this book the *black swan* or the *rare event*. Solon even understood another linked problem, which I call the *skewness* issue; it does not matter how frequently something succeeds if failure is too costly to bear.

Yet the story of Croesus has another twist. Having lost a battle to the redoubtable Persian king Cyrus, he was about to be burned alive when he called Solon's name and shouted (something like) "Solon, you were right" (again this is legend). Cyrus asked about the nature of such unusual invocations, and he told him about Solon's warning. This impressed Cyrus so much that he decided to spare Croesus' life, as he reflected on the possibilities as far as his own fate was concerned. People were thoughtful at that time.

ONE

IF YOU'RE SO RICH
WHY AREN'T YOU SO SMART?

An illustration of the effect of randomness on social pecking order and jealousy, through two characters of opposite attitudes. On the concealed rare event. How things in modern life may change rather rapidly, except, perhaps, in dentistry.

Nero Tulip

HIT BY LIGHTNING

Nero Tulip became obsessed with trading after witnessing a strange scene one spring day as he was visiting the Chicago Mercantile Exchange. A red convertible Porsche, driven at several times the city speed limit, abruptly stopped in front of the entrance, its tires emitting the sound of pigs being slaughtered. A visibly demented athletic man in his thirties, his face flushed red, emerged and ran up the steps as if he were chased by a tiger. He left the car double-parked, its engine running, provoking an angry fanfare of horns. After a long minute, a bored young man clad in a yellow jacket (yellow was the color reserved for clerks) came down the steps, visibly untroubled by the traffic commotion. He drove the car into the underground parking garage – perfunctorily as if it were his daily chore.

That day Nero Tulip was hit with what the French call a *coup de foudre*, a sudden intense (and obsessive) infatuation that strikes like lightning. "This is for me!", he screamed enthusiastically – he could not help comparing the life of a trader to the alternative lives that could present themselves to him. Academia conjured up the image of a silent university office with rude secretaries; business, the image of a quiet office staffed with slow thinkers and semi-slow thinkers who express themselves in full sentences.

TEMPORARY SANITY

Unlike a *coup de foudre*, the infatuation triggered by the Chicago scene has not left him close to a decade-and-a-half after the incident. For Nero swears that no other lawful profession in our times could be as devoid of boredom as that of the trader. Furthermore, although he has not yet practiced the profession of high-sea piracy, he is now convinced that even the occupation of pirate would present more dull moments than that of the trader.

Nero could best be described as someone who randomly (and abruptly) swings between the deportment and speech manners of a church historian and the verbally abusive intensity of a Chicago pit trader. He can commit hundreds of millions of dollars in a transaction without a blink or a shadow of second thoughts, yet agonize between two appetizers on the menu, changing his mind back and forth and wearing out the most patient of waiters.

Nero holds an undergraduate degree in ancient literature and mathematics from Cambridge University. He enrolled in a Ph.D. program in statistics at the University of Chicago but, after completing the prerequisite coursework, as well as the bulk of his doctoral research, he switched to the philosophy department. He called the switch "a moment of temporary sanity", adding to the consternation of his thesis director who warned him against philosophers and predicted his return back to the fold. He finished writing his thesis in philosophy. But not the Derrida continental style of incomprehensible philosophy (that is, *incomprehensible* to anyone outside of their ranks, like myself). It was quite the opposite; his thesis was on the methodology of statistical inference in its application to the social sciences. In fact, his thesis was indistinguishable from a thesis in mathematical statistics – it was just a bit more thoughtful (and twice as long).

It is often said that philosophy cannot feed its man – but that was not the reason Nero left. He left because philosophy cannot entertain its man. At first, it started looking futile; he recalled his statistics thesis director's warnings. Then, suddenly, it started to look like work. As he became tired of writing papers on some arcane details of his earlier papers, he gave up the academy. These academic debates bored him to tears, particularly when very small minute points (invisible to the non-initiated) were at stake. Action was what Nero required. The problem, however, was that he selected the academy in the first place in order to kill what he detected was the flatness and tempered submission of employment life.

After witnessing the scene of the trader chased by a tiger, Nero found a trainee spot on the Chicago Mercantile Exchange, the large exchange where traders transact by shouting and gesticulating frenetically. There he worked for a prestigious (but eccentric) *local*, who trained him in the Chicago style, in return for Nero solving his mathematical equations. The energy in the air proved motivating to Nero. He rapidly graduated to the rank of self-employed trader. Then, when he got tired of standing on his feet in the crowd, and straining his vocal cords, he decided to seek employment "upstairs", that is, trading from a desk. He moved to the New York area and took a position with an investment house.

Nero specialized in quantitative financial products, in which he had an early moment of glory, became famous and in demand. Many investment houses in New York and London flashed huge guaranteed bonuses at him. Nero spent a couple of years shuttling between New York and London, attending important "meetings" and wearing expensive suits. But soon Nero went into hiding; he rapidly pulled back to anonymity – the Wall Street stardom track did not quite fit his temperament. To stay a "hot trader" requires some organizational ambitions and a power hunger that he feels lucky not to possess. He was only in it for the fun – and his idea of fun does not include administrative and managerial work. He is susceptible to conference room boredom and is incapable of talking to businessmen, particularly those run-of-the-mill variety. Nero is allergic to the vocabulary of business talk, not just on plain aesthetic grounds. Words like "game plan", "bottom line", "how to get there from here", "we provide our clients with solutions", "our mission" and other hackneyed expressions that dominate meetings lack both the precision and the coloration that he prefers to hear. Whether people populate silence with hollow sentences, or if such meetings present any true merit, he does not know; at any rate he did not want to be part of it. Indeed Nero's extensive social life includes almost no business people. But unlike me (I can be extremely humiliating when someone rubs me the wrong way with inelegant pompousness), Nero handles himself with gentle aloofness in these circumstances.

So, Nero switched career to what is called proprietary trading. Traders are set up as independent entities, internal funds with their own allocation of capital. They are left alone to do as they please, provided of course that their results satisfy the executives. The name proprietary comes from the fact that they trade the company's own money. At the end of the year they receive between 7% and 12% of the profits generated. The proprietary trader has all the benefits of self employment, and none of the burdens of running the mundane details of his own business. He can work any hours he likes, can travel at a whim and engage in all manner of personal pursuits. It is paradise for an intellectual like Nero who dislikes manual work and values unscheduled meditation. He has been doing that for the past ten years, in the employment of two different trading firms.

MODUS OPERANDI

A word on Nero's methods. He is as conservative a trader as one can be in such a business. In the past he has had good years and less than good years – but virtually no truly "bad" years. Over these years he has slowly built for himself a stable nest egg, thanks to an income ranging between $300,000 and (at the peak) $2,500,000. On average, he manages to accumulate $500,000 a year in after-tax money (from an average income of about $1,000,000); this goes straight into his savings account. In 1993, he had a flat year and was made to feel uncomfortable in his company. Other traders made out much better, so the capital at his disposal was severely reduced, and he was made to feel undesirable at the institution. He then went to get an identical job, down to an identically designed workspace, but in a different firm that was friendlier. In the fall of 1994 the traders who had been competing for the great performance award blew up in unison during the worldwide bond market crash that resulted from the random tightening by the Federal Reserve Bank of the United States. They are all currently out of the market, performing a variety of tasks. This business has a high mortality rate.

Why doesn't Nero make more money? Because of his trading style – or perhaps his personality. His risk aversion is extreme. Nero's objective is not to maximize his profits, so much as it is to avoid having this entertaining money machine called trading taken away from him. Blowing up would mean returning to the tedium of the university or the non-trading life. Every time his risks increase, he conjures up the image of the quiet hallway at the university, the long mornings at his desk spent in revising a paper, kept awake by bad coffee. No, he does not want to have to face the solemn university library where he was bored to tears. "I am shooting for longevity", he is wont to say.

Nero has seen many traders *blow up*, and does not want to get into that situation. *Blow up* in the lingo has a precise meaning; it does not just mean to lose money; it means to lose more money than one ever expected, to the point of being thrown out of the business (the equivalent of a doctor losing his license to practice or a lawyer being disbarred). Nero rapidly exits trades after a predetermined loss. He never sells "naked options" (a strategy that would leave him exposed to large possible losses). He never puts himself in a situation where he can lose more than, say, $1,000,000 – regardless of the probability of such an event. That amount has always been variable; it depends on his accumulated profits for the year. This risk aversion prevented him from making as much money as the other traders on Wall Street who are often called "Masters of the Universe". The firms he has worked for generally allocate more money to traders with a different style, like John whom we will encounter soon.

Nero's temperament is such that he does not mind losing small money. "I love taking small losses", he says. "I just need my winners to be large". In no circumstances does he want to be exposed to those rare events, like panics and sudden crashes that wipe a trader out in a flash. To the contrary, he wants to benefit from them. When people ask him why he does not hold on to losers, he invariably answers that he was trained by "the most chicken of them all", the Chicago trader Stevo who taught him the business. This is not true; the real reason is his training in probability and his innate skepticism.

There is another reason why Nero is not as rich as others in his situation. His skepticism does not allow him to invest any of his own money outside of treasury bonds. He therefore missed out on the great bull market. The reason he offers is that it could have turned out to be a bear market and a trap. Nero harbors a deep suspicion that the stock market is some form of an investment scam and cannot bring himself to own a stock. The difference with people around him who were enriched by the stock market was that he was cash-flow rich, but his assets did not inflate at all along with the rest of the world (his treasury bonds hardly changed in value). He contrasts himself with one of those startup technology companies that were massively cash-flow negative, but for which the hordes developed some infatuation. This allowed the owners to become rich from their stock valuation, and thus dependent on the randomness of the market's election of the winner. The difference with his friends of the investing variety is that he did not depend on the bull market, and, accordingly, does not have to worry about a bear market at all. His net worth is not a function of the investment of his savings – he does not want to depend on his investments, but on his cash earnings, for his enrichment. He takes not an inch of risk with his savings, which he invests in the safest possible vehicles. Treasury bonds are safe; they are issued by the United States Government, and governments can hardly go bankrupt since they can freely print their own currency to pay back their obligation.

NO WORK ETHICS

Today, at 39, after 14 years in the business, he can consider himself comfortably settled. His personal portfolio contains several million dollars in medium maturity Treasury Bonds, enough to eliminate any worry about the future. What he likes most about proprietary trading is that it requires considerably less time than other high-paying professions; in other words it is perfectly compatible with his non-middle-class work ethics. Trading forces someone to think hard; those who merely work hard generally lose their focus and intellectual energy. In addition, they end up drowning in randomness; work ethics, Nero believes, draw people to focus on noise rather than the signal (the difference we established in Table P.1 on page 3).

This free time has allowed him to carry on a variety of personal interests. As Nero reads voraciously and spends considerable time in the gym and museums, he cannot have a lawyer's or a doctor's schedule. Nero found the time to go back to the statistics department where he started his doctoral studies and finished the "harder science" doctorate in statistics, by rewriting his thesis in more concise terms. Nero now teaches, once a year, a half-semester seminar called *History of Probabilistic Thinking* in the mathematics department of New York University, a class of great originality that draws excellent graduate students. He has saved enough money to be able to maintain his lifestyle in the future and has contingency plans perhaps to retire into writing popular essays of the scientific-literary variety, with themes revolving around probability and *indeterminism* – but only if some event in the future causes the markets to shut down.

THERE ARE ALWAYS SECRETS

Nero's probabilistic introspection may have been helped out by some dramatic event in his life – one that he kept to himself. A penetrating observer might detect in Nero a measure of suspicious exuberance, an unnatural drive. For his life is not as crystalline as it may seem. Nero harbors a secret, one that will be discussed in time.

John the High-Yield Trader

Through most of the 1990s, across the street from Nero's house stood John's – a much larger one. John was a high-yield trader, but he was not a trader in the style of Nero. A brief professional conversation with him would have revealed that he presented the intellectual depth and sharpness of mind of an aerobics instructor (though not the physique). A purblind man could have seen that John had been doing markedly better than Nero (or, at least, felt compelled to show it). He parked two top-of-the-line German cars in his driveway (his and hers), in addition to two convertibles (one of which was a collectible Ferrari), while Nero had been driving the same VW cabriolet for almost a decade – and still does.

The wives of John and Nero were acquaintances, of the health-club type of acquaintance, but Nero's wife felt extremely uncomfortable in the company of John's. She felt that the lady was not merely trying to impress her, but was treating her like someone inferior. While Nero had become inured to the sight of traders getting rich (and trying too hard to become sophisticated by turning into wine collectors and opera lovers), his wife had rarely encountered repressed new wealth – the type of people who have felt the sting of indigence at some point in their lives and want to get even by exhibiting their wares. The only dark side of being a trader, Nero often says, is the sight of money being showered on unprepared people who are suddenly taught that Vivaldi's *Four Seasons* is "refined" music. But it was hard for his spouse to be exposed almost daily to the neighbor who kept boasting of the new decorator they just hired. John and his wife were not the least uncomfortable with the fact that their "library" came with the leather-bound books (her readings at the health club was limited to *People Magazine* but her shelves included a selection of untouched books by dead American authors). She also kept discussing unpronounceable exotic locations where they would repair during their vacations without so much as knowing the smallest thing about the place – she would have been hard put to explain in which continent the Seychelles Islands were located. Nero's wife is all too human; although she kept telling herself that she did not want to be in the shoes of John's wife, she felt as if she had been somewhat swamped in the competition of life. Somehow words and reason became ineffectual in front of an oversized diamond, a monstrous house, and a sports car collection.

AN OVERPAID HICK

Nero also suffered the same ambiguous feeling towards his neighbors. He was quite contemptuous of John, who represented about everything he is not and does not want to be – but there was the social pressure that was starting to weigh in on him. In addition, he too would like to have sampled such excessive wealth. Intellectual contempt does not control personal envy. That house across the street kept getting bigger, with addition after addition – and Nero's discomfort kept apace. While Nero had succeeded beyond his wildest dreams, both personally and intellectually, he was starting to consider himself as having missed a chance somewhere. In the pecking order of Wall Street, the arrival of such types as John had caused him no longer to be a significant trader – but while he used to not care about this, John and his house and his cars had started to gnaw away at him. All would have been well if Nero had not had that stupid large house across the street judging him with a superficial standard every morning. Was it the genetic pecking order at play, with John's house size making him a beta male? Worse even, John was about five years his junior, and, despite a shorter career, was making at least ten times his income.

When they used to run into each other Nero had a clear feeling that John tried to put him down – with barely detectable but no less potent signs of condescension. Some days John ignored him completely. Had John been a remote character, one Nero could only read about in the papers, the situation would have been different. But there John was in flesh and bones and he was his neighbor. The mistake Nero made was to start talking to him, as the rule of pecking order immediately emerged. Nero tried to soothe his discomfort by recalling the behavior of Swann, the character in Proust's *In Search of Time Lost*, a refined art dealer and man of leisure who was at ease with such men as his personal friend the then Prince of Wales, but acted like he had to prove something in the presence of the middle class. It was much easier for Swann to mix with the aristocratic and well established set of Guermantes than it was with the social-climbing one of the Verdurins, no doubt because he was far more confident in their presence. Likewise Nero can exact some form of respect from prestigious and prominent people. He regularly takes long meditative walks in Paris and Venice with an erudite Nobel prize-caliber scientist (the kind of person who no longer has to prove anything) who actively seeks his conversation. A very famous billionaire speculator calls him regularly to ask him his opinion on the valuation of some derivative securities. But there he was obsessively trying to gain the respect of some overpaid hick with a cheap New Jersey "Noo-Joyzy" accent. (Had I been in Nero's shoes I would have paraded some of my scorn to John with the use of body language, but again, Nero is a nice person.)

Clearly, John was not as well educated, well bred, physically fit, or perceived as being as intelligent as Nero – but that was not all; he was not even as street-smart as him! Nero has met true street-smart people in the pits of Chicago who exhibit a rapidity of thinking that he could not detect in John. Nero was convinced that the man was a confident shallow-thinker who had done well because he never made an allowance for his vulnerability. But Nero could not, at times, repress his envy – he wondered whether it was an objective evaluation of John, or if it was his feelings of being slighted that led him to such an assessment of John. Perhaps it was Nero who was not quite the best trader. Maybe if he had pushed himself harder or had sought the right opportunity – instead of "thinking", writing articles and reading complicated papers. Perhaps he should have been involved in the high-yield business, where he would have shined among those shallow-thinkers like John.

So Nero tried to soothe his jealousy by investigating the rules of pecking order. Psychologists Kahneman and Tversky showed that most people prefer to make $70,000 when others around them are making $60,000 than to make $80,000 when others around them are making $90,000. Economics, schmeconomics, it is all pecking order, he thought. No such analysis could prevent him from assessing his condition in an absolute rather than a relative way. With John, Nero felt that, for all his intellectual training, he was just another one of those who would prefer to make less money provided others made even less.

Nero thought that there was at least one piece of evidence to support the idea of John being merely lucky – in other words Nero, after all, might not need to move away from his neighbor's starter palazzo. There was hope that John would meet his undoing. For John seemed unaware of one large hidden risk he was taking, the risk of blow up, a risk he could not see because he had too short an experience of the market (but also because he was not thoughtful enough to study history). How could

John, with his coarse mind, otherwise be making so much money? This business of junk bonds depends on some knowledge of the "odds", a calculation of the probability of the rare (or random) events. What do such fools know about odds? These traders use "quantitative tools" that give them the odds – and Nero disagrees with the methods used. This high-yield market resembles a nap on a railway track. One afternoon, the surprise train would run you over. You make money every month for a long time, then lose a multiple of your cumulative performance in a few hours. He has seen it with option sellers in 1987, 1989, 1992, and 1998. One day they are taken off the exchange floors, accompanied by oversized security men, and nobody ever sees them again. The big house is simply a loan; John might end up as a luxury car salesman somewhere in New Jersey, selling to the new newly rich who no doubt would feel comfortable in his presence. Nero cannot blow up. His less oversized abode, with its 4,000 books, is his own. No market event can take it away from him. Every one of his losses is limited. His trader's dignity will never, never, be threatened.

John, for his part, thought of Nero as a loser, and a snobbish over-educated loser at that. Nero was involved in a mature business. He believed that he was way over the hill. "These 'prop' traders are dying", he used to say. "They think they are smarter than everybody else, but they are *passé*".

The Red-Hot Summer

Finally, in September 1998, Nero was vindicated. One morning while leaving to go to work he saw John in his front yard unusually smoking a cigarette. He was not wearing a business suit. He looked humble; his customary swagger was gone. Nero immediately knew that John had been fired. What he did not suspect was that John also lost almost everything he had. We will see more details of John's losses in Chapter 5.

Nero felt ashamed of his feelings of *schadenfreude*, the joy humans can experience upon their rivals' misfortune. But he could not repress it. Aside from it being unchivalrous, it was said to bring bad luck (Nero is weakly superstitious). But in this case, Nero's merriment did not come from the fact that John went back to his place in life, so much as it was from the fact that Nero's methods, beliefs, and track record had suddenly gained in credibility. Nero would be able to raise public money on his track record precisely because such a thing could not possibly happen to him. A repetition of such an event would pay off massively for him. Part of Nero's elation also came from the fact that he felt proud of his sticking to his strategy for so long, in spite of the pressure to be the alpha male. It was also because he would no longer question his trading style when others were getting rich because they misunderstood the structure of randomness and market cycles.

SEROTONIN AND RANDOMNESS

Can we judge the success of people by their raw performance and their personal wealth? Sometimes – but not always. We will see how, at any point in time, a large section of businessmen with outstanding track records will be no better than randomly thrown darts. More curiously, and owing to a peculiar bias, cases will abound of the least-skilled businessmen being the richest. However, they will fail to make an allowance for the role of luck in their performance.

Lucky fools do not bear the slightest suspicion that they may be lucky fools – by definition, they do not know that they belong to such category. They will act as if they deserved the money. Their strings of successes will inject them with so much *serotonin* (or some similar substance) that they will even fool themselves about their ability to outperform markets (our hormonal system does not know whether our successes depend on randomness). One can notice it in their posture; a profitable trader will walk upright, dominant style – and will tend to talk more than a losing trader. Scientists found out that serotonin, a neurotransmitter, seems to command a large share of our human behavior. It sets a positive feedback, the virtuous circle, but, owing to an external kick from randomness, can start a reverse motion and cause a vicious circle. It has been shown that monkeys injected with serotonin will rise in the pecking order, which in turn causes an increase of the serotonin level in their blood – until the virtuous cycle breaks and starts a vicious one (during the vicious cycle failure will cause one to slide in the pecking order, causing a behavior that will bring about further drops in the pecking order). Likewise, an increase in personal performance (regardless of whether it is caused deterministically or by the agency of lady Fortuna) induces a rise of serotonin in the subject, itself causing an increase of what is commonly called *leadership* ability. One is "on a roll". Some imperceptible changes in deportment, like an ability to express oneself with serenity and confidence, makes the subject look credible – as if he truly deserved the shekels. Randomness will be ruled out as a possible factor in the performance, until it rears its head once again and delivers the kick that will induce the vicious cycle.

People have often had the bad taste of asking me in a social setting if my day in trading was profitable. If my father were there, he would usually stop them by saying "never ask a man if he is from Sparta: if he were, he would have let you know such an important fact – and if he were not, you could hurt his feelings". Likewise, never ask a trader if he is profitable; you can easily see it in his gesture and gait. People in the profession can easily tell if traders are making or losing money; head traders are quick at identifying an employee who is faring poorly. Their face will seldom reveal much, as people consciously attempt to gain control of their facial expressions. But the way they walk, the way they hold the telephone, and the hesitation in their behavior, will not fail to reveal their true disposition. On the morning after John had been fired, he certainly lost much of his serotonin – unless it was another substance that researchers will discover in another decade. One cab driver in Chicago explained to me that he could tell if traders he picked up near the Chicago Board of Trade, a futures exchange, were doing well. "They get all puffed up", he said. I found it interesting (and mysterious) that he could detect it so rapidly. I later got some plausible explanation from evolutionary psychology, which claims that such physical manifestations of one's performance in life, just like an animal's dominant condition, can be used for signaling: it makes the winners seem easily visible, which is efficient in mate selection.

Your Dentist Is Rich, Very Rich

We close this chapter with a hint on the next discussion of resistance to randomness. Recall that Nero can considered prosperous but not "very rich" by his day's standards. However, according to some strange accounting measure we will see in the next chapter, he is extremely rich *on the average of lives* he could have led – he takes so little risk in his trading career that there could have been very few disastrous outcomes. The fact that he did not experience John's success was the reason he did not suffer his downfall. He would be therefore wealthy according to this unusual (and probabilistic) method of accounting for wealth. Recall that Nero protects himself from the rare event. Had Nero had to relive his professional life a few million times, very few sample paths would be marred by bad luck – but, owing to his conservatism, very few as well would be affected by extreme good luck. That is, his life in stability would be similar to that of an ecclesiastic clock repairman. Naturally, we are discussing only his professional life, excluding his (sometimes volatile) private one.

Arguably, *in expectation*, a dentist is considerably richer than the rock musician who is driven in a pink Rolls Royce, the speculator who bids up the price of impressionist paintings, or the entrepreneur who collects private jets. For one cannot consider a profession without taking into account the average of the people who enter it, not the sample of those who have succeeded in it. We will examine the point later from the vantage point of the survivorship bias, but here, in Part I, we will look at it with respect to resistance to randomness.

Consider two neighbors, John Doe A, a janitor who won the New Jersey lottery and moved to a wealthy neighborhood, compared to John Doe B, his next-door neighbor of more modest condition who has been drilling teeth eight hours a day over the past 35 years. Clearly one can say that, thanks to the dullness of his career, if John Doe B had to relive his life a few thousand times since graduation from dental school, the range of possible outcomes would be rather narrow (assuming he is properly insured). At the best, he would end up drilling the rich teeth of the New York Park Avenue residents, while the worst would show him drilling those of some semi-deserted town full of trailers in the Catskills.

Furthermore, assuming he graduated from a very prestigious teeth-drilling school, the range of outcomes would be even more compressed. As to John Doe A, if he had to relive his life a million times, almost all of them would see him performing janitorial activities (and spending endless dollars on fruitless lottery tickets), and one in a million would see him winning the New Jersey lottery.

The idea of taking into account both the observed and unobserved possible outcomes sounds like lunacy. For most people, probability is about what may happen in the future, not events in the observed past; an event that has already taken place has 100% probability, i.e., certainty. I have discussed the point with many people who platitudinously accuse me of confusing myth and reality. Myths, particularly well-aged ones, as we saw with Solon's warning, can be far more potent (and provide us with more experience) than plain reality.

TWO

A BIZARRE ACCOUNTING METHOD

*On alternative histories, a probabilistic view of the world,
intellectual fraud, and the randomness wisdom of a Frenchman
with steady bathing habits. How journalists are bred to not
understand random series of events. Beware borrowed wisdom:
how almost all great ideas concerning random outcomes are
against conventional sapience. On the difference between
correctness and intelligibility.*

Alternative History

I start with the platitude that one cannot judge a performance in any
given field (war, politics, medicine, investments) by the results, but by
the costs of the alternative (i.e. if history played out in a different way).
Such substitute courses of events are called *alternative histories*. Clearly,
the quality of a decision cannot be solely judged based on its outcome,
but such a point seems to be voiced only by people who fail (those who
succeed attribute their success to the quality of their decision). Such
opinion is what politicians on their way out of office keep telling those
members of the press who still listen to them that they followed the best

course – eliciting the customary commiserating "yes, we know" that makes the sting even worse. And like many platitudes, this one, while being too obvious, is not easy to carry out in practice.

RUSSIAN ROULETTE

One can illustrate the strange concept of alternative histories as follows. Imagine an eccentric (and bored) tycoon offering you $10 million to play Russian roulette, i.e. to put a revolver containing one bullet in the six available chambers to your head and pull the trigger. Each realization would count as one history, for a total of six possible histories of equal probabilities. Five out of these six histories would lead to enrichment; one would lead to a statistic, that is, an obituary with an embarrassing (but certainly original) cause of death. The problem is that only one of the histories is observed in reality; and the winner of $10 million would elicit the admiration and praise of some fatuous journalist (the very same ones who unconditionally admire the Forbes 500 billionaires). Like almost every executive I have encountered during a 15-year career on Wall Street (the role of such executives in my view being no more than a judge of results delivered in a random manner), the public observes the external signs of wealth without even having a glimpse at the source (we call such source the *generator*). Consider the possibility that the Russian roulette winner would be used as a role model by his family, friends, and neighbors.

While the remaining five histories are not observable, the wise and thoughtful person could easily make a guess as to their attributes. It requires some thoughtfulness and personal courage. In addition, in time, if the roulette-betting fool keeps playing the game, the bad histories will tend to catch up with him. Thus, if a 25-year-old played Russian roulette, say, once a year, there would be a very slim possibility of his surviving his 50th birthday – but, if there are enough players, say thousands of 25-year-old players, we can expect to see a handful of (extremely rich) survivors (and a very large cemetery). Here I have to admit that the example of Russian roulette is more than intellectual to me. I lost a comrade to this "game" during the Lebanese war, when we were in our teens. But there is more. I discovered that I had more than a shallow interest in literature thanks to the effect of Graham Greene's account of his flirt with such a game; it bore a stronger effect on me than the actual events I had recently witnessed. Greene claimed that he once tried to soothe the dullness of his childhood by pulling the trigger on a revolver – making me shiver at the thought that I had at least a one in six probability of having been without his novels.

The reader can see my unusual notion of alternative accounting: $10 million earned through Russian roulette does not have the same value as $10 million earned through the diligent and artful practice of dentistry. They are the same, can buy the same goods, except that one's dependence on randomness is greater than the other. To an accountant, though, they would be identical. To your next-door neighbor too. Yet, deep down, I cannot help but consider them as qualitatively different. The notion of such alternative accounting has interesting intellectual extensions and lends itself to mathematical formulation, as we will see in the next chapter with our introduction of the Monte Carlo engine. Note that such use of mathematics is only illustrative, aiming at getting the intuition of the point, and should not be interpreted as an engineering issue. In other words, one need not actually compute the alternative histories so much as assess their attributes. Mathematics is not just a "numbers game", it is a way of thinking. We will see that probability is a qualitative subject.

AN EVEN MORE VICIOUS ROULETTE

Reality is far more vicious than Russian roulette. First, it delivers the fatal bullet rather infrequently, like a revolver that would have hundreds, even thousands of chambers instead of six. After a few dozen tries, one forgets about the existence of a bullet, under a numbing false sense of security. The point is dubbed in this book the *black swan problem*, which we cover in Chapter 7, as it is linked to the problem of induction, a problem that has kept a few philosophers of science awake at night. It is also related to a problem called *denigration of history* as gamblers, investors, and decision makers feel that the sort of things that happen to others would not necessarily happen to them.

Second, unlike a well-defined precise game like Russian roulette, where the risks are visible to anyone capable of multiplying and dividing by six, one does not observe the barrel of reality. Very rarely is the generator visible to the naked eye. One is thus capable of unwittingly playing Russian roulette – and calling it by some alternative "low risk" name. We see the wealth being generated, never the processor, a matter that makes people lose sight of their risks, and never the losers. The game seems terribly easy and we play along blithely.

Smooth Peer Relations

The degree of resistance to randomness in one's life is an abstract idea, part of its logic counterintuitive, and, to confuse matters, its realizations non-observable. But I have been increasingly devoted to it – for a collection of personal reasons I will leave for later. Clearly my way of judging matters is probabilistic in nature; it relies on the notion of what could have *probably* happened, and requires a certain mental attitude with respect to one's observations. I do not recommend engaging an accountant in a discussion about such probabilistic considerations. For an accountant a number is a number. If he were interested in probability he would have gotten involved in more introspective professions – and would be inclined to make a costly mistake on your tax return.

While we do not see the roulette barrel of reality, some people give it a try; it takes a special mindset to do so. Having seen hundreds of people enter and exit my profession (characterized by extreme dependence on randomness), I have to say that those who have had a modicum of scientific training tend to go the extra mile. For many, such thinking is second nature. This might not necessarily come from their scientific training *per se* (beware of causality), but possibly from the fact that people who have decided at some point in their lives to devote themselves to scientific research tend to have an ingrained intellectual curiosity and a natural tendency for such introspection. Particularly thoughtful are those who had to abandon scientific studies because of their inability to keep focused on a narrowly defined problem. Without excessive intellectual curiosity it is almost impossible to complete a Ph.D. thesis these days, but without a desire to narrowly specialize it is impossible to make a scientific career. (There is a distinction, however, between the mind of a pure mathematician thriving on abstraction and that of a scientist consumed by curiosity. A mathematician is absorbed in what goes into his head while a scientist searches into what is outside of himself.) However, some people's concern for randomness can be excessive; I have even seen people trained in some fields, like say, quantum mechanics, push the idea to the other extreme, only seeing alternative histories and ignoring the one that actually took place.

Some traders can be unexpectedly introspective about randomness. I recently had dinner at the bar of the Odeon with Lauren R., a trader who was reading a draft of this book. We flipped a coin to see who was going to pay for the meal. I lost and paid. He was about to thank me when he abruptly stopped and said: "Reading your book you would say that I paid for half of it probabilistically".

I thus view people distributed across two polar categories: on one extreme, those who never accept the notion of randomness; on the other, those who are tortured by it. When I started on Wall Street in the 1980s, trading rooms were populated with people with a "business orientation", that is, generally devoid of any introspection, flat as a pancake, and likely to be fooled by randomness. Their failure rate was extremely high, particularly when financial instruments gained in complexity. Somehow tricky products, like exotic options, were introduced and carried counterintuitive payoffs that were too difficult for someone of such culture to handle. They dropped like flies; I do not think that many of the hundreds of MBAs of my generation I met on Wall Street in the 1980s still engage in such forms of professional and disciplined risk taking.

SALVATION VIA AEROFLOT

The 1990s witnessed the arrival of people of richer and more interesting backgrounds, which made the trading rooms far more entertaining. I was saved from the conversation of MBAs. Many scientists, some of them extremely successful in their field, arrived with a desire to make a buck. They, in turn, hired people who resembled them. While most of these people were not Ph.D.s (indeed, the Ph.D. is still a minority), the culture and values suddenly changed, becoming more tolerant of intellectual depth. It caused an increase in the already high demand for scientists on Wall Street, owing to the rapid development of financial instruments. The dominant specialty was physics, but one could find all manner of quantitative backgrounds among them. Russian, French, Chinese, and Indian accents (by order) began dominating in both New York and London. It was said that every plane from Moscow had at least its back row full of Russian mathematical physicists *en route* to Wall Street (they lacked the street smarts to get good seats). One could hire very cheap labor by going to JFK airport with a (mandatory) translator, randomly interviewing those that fitted the stereotype. Indeed, by the late 1990s one could get someone trained by a world-class scientist for almost half the price of an MBA. As they say, marketing is everything; these guys do not know how to sell themselves.

I had a strong bias in favor of Russian scientists; many can be put to active use as chess coaches (I also got a piano teacher out of the process). In addition, they are extremely helpful in the interview process. When MBAs apply for trading positions, they frequently boast "advanced" chess skills on their résumés. I recall the MBA career counselor at Wharton recommending our advertising chess skills "because it sounds intelligent and strategic". MBAs, typically, can interpret their superficial knowledge of the rules of the game into "expertise". We used to verify the accuracy of claims of chess expertise (and the character of the applicant) by pulling a chess set out of a drawer and telling the student, now turning pale: "Yuri will have a word with you".

The failure rate of these scientists, though, was better, but only slightly so than that of MBAs; but it came from another reason, linked to their being on average (but only on average) devoid of the smallest bit of practical intelligence. Some successful scientists had the judgment (and social graces) of a door knob – but by no means all of them. Many people were capable of the most complex calculations with utmost rigor when it came to equations, but were totally incapable of solving a problem with the smallest connection to reality; it was as if they understood the letter but not the spirit of the math. I am convinced that X, a likeable Russian man of my acquaintance, has two brains: one for math and another, considerably inferior one, for everything else (which included solving problems related to the mathematics of finance). But on occasion a fast-thinking scientific-minded person with street smarts would emerge. Whatever the benefits of such population shift, it improved our chess skills and provided us with quality conversation during lunchtime – it extended the lunch hour considerably. Consider that I had in the 1980s to chat with colleagues who had an MBA or tax accounting background and were capable of the heroic feat of discussing FASB standards. I have to say that their interests were not too contagious. The interesting thing about these physicists does not lie in their ability to discuss fluid dynamics; it is that they were naturally interested in a variety of intellectual subjects and provide pleasant conversation.

SOLON VISITS *REGINE'S* NIGHT CLUB

As the reader may already suspect, my opinions about randomness have not earned me the smoothest of relations with some of my peers during my Wall Street career (many of whom the reader can see indirectly – but only indirectly – portrayed in these chapters). But where I had uneven relations was with some of those who had the misfortune of being my bosses. For I had two bosses in my life of contrasting characteristics in about every trait.

The first, whom I will call Kenny, was the epitome of the suburban family man. He would be of the type to coach soccer on Saturday morning, and invite his brother-in-law for a Sunday afternoon barbecue. He gave the appearance of someone I would trust with my savings – indeed he rose quite rapidly in the institution in spite of his lack of technical competence in financial derivatives (his firm's claim to fame). But he was too much a no-nonsense person to make out my logic. He once blamed me for not being impressed with the successes of some of his traders who did well during the bull market for European bonds of 1993, whom I openly considered nothing better than random gunslingers. I tried presenting him with the notion of survivorship bias (Part II of this book) in vain. His traders have all exited the business since then "to pursue other interests" (including him). But he gave the appearance of being a calm, measured man, who spoke his mind and knew how to put the other person at ease during a conversation. He was articulate, extremely presentable thanks to his athletic looks, well measured in his speech, and was endowed with the extremely rare quality of being an excellent listener. His personal charm allowed him to win the confidence of the chairman – but I could not conceal my disrespect, particularly as he could not make out the nature of my conversation. In spite of his conservative looks he was a perfect time bomb, ticking away.

The second, whom I will call Jean-Patrice, in contrast, was a moody Frenchman with an explosive temper and a hyper-aggressive personality. Except for those he truly liked (not that many), he was expert at making his subordinates uncomfortable, putting them in a state of constant anxiety. He greatly contributed to my formation as a risk-taker; he is one of the very rare people who have the guts to care only about the generator, entirely oblivious of the results. He presented the wisdom of Solon, but, while one would expect someone with such personal wisdom and such understanding of randomness to lead a dull life, he lived a colorful one. In contrast with Kenny, who wore conservative dark suits and white shirts (his only indulgence was flashy equestrian Hermes ties), Jean-Patrice dressed like a peacock: blue shirts, plaid sports coats stuffed with gaudy silk pocket squares. No family-minded man, he rarely came to work before noon – though I can safely say that he carried his work with him to the most unlikely places. He frequently called me from *Regine's*, an upscale night-club in New York, waking me up at three in the morning to discuss some small (and irrelevant) details of my risk exposure. In spite of his slight corpulence, women seemed to find him irresistible; he frequently disappeared at midday and was unreachable for hours. His advantage might have been in his being a New York Frenchman with steady bathing habits. Once, recently, he invited me to discuss an urgent business issue with him. Characteristically, I found him mid-afternoon in a strange "club" in Paris that carried no nameplate and where he sat with documents strewn across the table from him. Sipping champagne, he was simultaneously caressed by two scantily dressed young ladies. Strangely, he involved them in the conversation as if they were part of the meeting. He even had one of the ladies pick up his constantly ringing mobile phone as he did not want our conversation to be interrupted.

I am still amazed at this flamboyant man's obsession with risks, which he constantly played in his head – he literally thought of everything that could possibly happen. He forced me to make an alternative plan should a plane crash into the office building – and fumed at my answer that the financial condition of his department would be of small interest to me in such circumstances. He had a horrible reputation as a philanderer, a temperamental boss capable of firing someone at a whim, yet he listened to me and understood every word I had to say, encouraging me to go the extra mile in my study of randomness. He taught me to look for the invisible risks of blowup in any portfolio. Not coincidentally, he has an immense respect for science and an almost fawning deference for scientists; a decade or so after we worked together he showed up unexpectedly during the defense of my doctoral thesis, smiling from the back of the room. While Kenny knew how to climb the ladder of an institution, reaching a high level in the organization before being forced out, Jean-Patrice did not have such a happy career, a matter that taught me to beware of mature financial institutions.

It can be disturbing for many self-styled "bottom line" oriented people to be questioned about the histories that did not take place rather than the ones that actually happened. Clearly, to a no-nonsense person of the "successful in business" variety, my language (and, I have to reckon, some traits of my personality) appear strange and incomprehensible. To my amusement, the argument appears offensive to many.

The contrast between Kenny and Jean-Patrice is not a mere coincidence in a protracted career. Beware the spendthrift "businesswise" person; the cemetery of markets is disproportionately well stocked with the self-styled "bottom line" people. In contrast with their customary Masters of the Universe demeanor, they suddenly look pale, humble and hormone-deprived on the way to the personnel office for the customary discussion of the severance agreement.

George Will Is No Solon: On Counterintuitive Truths

Realism can be punishing. Probabilistic skepticism is worse. It is difficult to go about life wearing probabilistic glasses, as one starts seeing fools of randomness all around, in a variety of situations – obdurate in their perceptional illusion. To start, it is impossible to read a historian's analysis without questioning the inferences: we know that Hannibal and Hitler were mad in their pursuits, as Rome is not today Phoenician-speaking and Times Square in New York currently exhibits no swastikas. But what of all those generals who were equally foolish, but ended up winning the war and consequently the esteem of the historical chronicler? It is hard to think of Alexander the Great or Julius Caesar as men who won only in the visible history, but who could have suffered defeat in others. If we have heard of them, it is simply because they took considerable risks, along with thousands of others and happened to win. They were intelligent, courageous, noble (at times), had the highest possible obtainable culture in their day – but so did thousands of others who live in the musty footnotes of history. Again I am not contesting that they won their wars – only the claims concerning the quality of their strategies. (My very first impression upon a recent rereading of the *Iliad*, the first in my adulthood, is that the epic poet did not judge his heroes by the result: heroes won and lost battles in a manner that was totally independent of their own valor; their fate depended upon totally external forces, generally the explicit agency of the scheming gods (not devoid of nepotism). Heroes are heroes because they are heroic in behavior, not because they won or lost. Patrocles does not strike us as a hero because of his accomplishments (he was rapidly killed) but because he preferred to die than see Achilles sulking into inaction. Clearly the epic poets understood invisible histories. Also later thinkers and poets had more elaborate methods for dealing with randomness, as we will see with stoicism.)

Listening to the media, mostly because I am not used to it, can cause me on occasion to jump out of my seat and become emotional in front of the moving image (I grew up with no television and was in my late twenties when I learned to operate a TV set). One illustration of a dangerous refusal to consider alternative histories is provided by the interview that media person George Will, a "commentator" of the extensively commenting variety, conducted with Professor Robert Shiller, a man known to the public for his best-selling book *Irrational Exuberance*, but known to the connoisseur for his remarkable insights about the structure of market randomness and volatility (expressed in the precision of mathematics).

The interview is illustrative of the destructive aspect of the media, in catering to our heavily warped common sense and biases. I was told that George Will was very famous and extremely respected (that is, for a journalist). He might even be someone of utmost intellectual integrity; his profession, however, is merely to sound smart and intelligent to the hordes. Shiller, on the other hand, understands the ins and outs of randomness; he is trained to deal with rigorous argumentation, but does sound less smart in public because his subject matter is highly counterintuitive. Shiller had been pronouncing the stock market to be overpriced for a long time. George Will indicated to Shiller that had people listened to him in the past they would have lost money, as the market has more than doubled since he started pronouncing it overvalued. To such a journalistic and well sounding (but senseless) argument, Shiller was unable to respond except to explain that the fact that he was wrong in one single market call should not carry undue significance. Shiller, as a scientist, did not claim being a prophet or one of the entertainers who comment on the markets on the evening news. Yogi Berra would have had a better time with his confident comment on the fat lady not having sung yet.

I could not understand what Shiller, untrained to compress his ideas into vapid sound-bites, was doing on such a TV show. Clearly, it is foolish to think that an irrational market cannot become even more irrational; Shiller's views on the rationality of the market are not invalidated by the argument that he was wrong in the past. Here I could not help seeing in the person of George Will the representative of so many nightmares in my career; my attempting to prevent someone from playing Russian roulette for $10 million and seeing journalist George Will humiliating me in public by saying that had the person listened to me it would have cost him a considerable fortune. In addition, Will's comment was not an off-the-cuff remark; he wrote an article on the matter discussing Shiller's bad "prophecy". Such tendency to make and unmake prophets based on the fate of the roulette wheel is symptomatic of our genetic inability to cope with the complex structure of randomness prevailing in the modern world. Mixing forecast and prophecy is symptomatic of randomness foolishness (prophecy belongs to the right column, forecast is its mere left-column equivalent).

HUMILIATED IN DEBATES

Clearly, this idea of alternative history does not make intuitive sense, which is where the fun begins. For starters, we are not wired in a way to understand probability, a point that we will examine backward and forward in this book. I will just say at this point that researchers of the brain believe that mathematical truths make little sense to our mind, particularly when it comes to the examination of random outcomes. Most results in probability are entirely counterintuitive; we will see plenty of them. Then why argue with a mere journalist whose paycheck comes from playing on the conventional wisdom of the hordes? I recall that every time I have been humiliated in a public discussion on markets by someone (of the George Will variety) who seemed to present more palatable and easier to understand arguments, I turned out (much later) to be right. I do not dispute that arguments should be simplified to their maximum potential; but people often confuse complex ideas that cannot be simplified into a media-friendly statement as symptomatic of a confused mind. MBAs learn the concept of clarity and simplicity, the five-minute-manager take on things. The concept may apply to the business plan for a fertilizer plant, but not to highly probabilistic arguments – which is the reason I have anecdotal evidence in my business that MBAs tend to blow up in financial markets, as they are trained to simplify matters a couple of steps beyond their requirement (I beg the MBA reader not to take offense; I am myself the unhappy holder of the degree).

Beware the confusion between correctness and intelligibility. Part of conventional wisdom favors things that can be explained rather instantly and "in a nutshell" – in many circles it is considered law. Having attended a French elementary school, a *lycée primaire*, I was trained to rehash the popular adage:

Ce qui se conçoit bien s'énonce clairement
Et les mots pour le dire viennent aisément

What is easy to conceive is clear to express/Words to say it would come effortlessly.

The reader can imagine my disappointment at realizing, while growing up as a practitioner of randomness, that most poetic sounding adages are plain wrong. Borrowed wisdom can be vicious. I need to make a huge effort not to be swayed by well-sounding remarks. I remind myself of Einstein's remark that common sense is nothing but a collection of misconceptions acquired by age 18. Furthermore: *what sounds intelligent in a conversation or a meeting, or, particularly in the media, is suspicious.*

Any reading of the history of science would show that almost all the smart things that have been proven by science appeared like lunacies at the time they were first discovered. Try to explain to a *London Times* journalist in 1905 that time slows down when one travels (even the Nobel committee never granted Einstein the prize on account of his insight on special relativity). Or to someone with no exposure to physics that there are places in our universe where time does not exist. Try to explain to Kenny that, although his star trader had made him a lot of money, I have enough arguments to convince him that he is a dangerous idiot.

RISK MANAGERS

Corporations and financial institutions have recently created the strange position of risk manager, someone who is supposed to monitor the institution and verify that it is not too deeply involved in the business of playing Russian roulette. Clearly, having been burned a few times, the incentive is there to have someone take a look at the generator, the roulette that produces the profits and losses. Although it is more fun to trade, many extremely smart people among my friends (including Jean-Patrice) felt attracted by such positions. It is an important and attractive fact that the average risk manager earns more than the average trader (particularly when we take into account the number of traders thrown out of the business). But their job feels strange, for the following reason: as we said, the generator of reality is not observable. They are limited in their power to stop profitable traders from taking risks, given that they would, *ex post* be accused by the George Wills around of costing the shareholder some precious opportunity shekels. On the other hand, the occurrence of a blowup would cause them to be responsible for it. What to do in such circumstances?

Their focus becomes to play politics, cover themselves by issuing vaguely phrased internal memoranda that warn against risk-taking activities yet stop short of completely condemning it, lest they lose their job. Like a doctor torn between the two types of errors, the false positive (telling the patient he has cancer when in fact he does not) and the false negative (telling the patient he is healthy when in fact he has cancer), they need to balance their existence with the fact that they inherently need some margin of error in their business. For my part, I resolved the problem long ago by being both the risk manager and the boss at my current operation.

I conclude the chapter with a presentation of the central paradox of my career in financial randomness. By definition, I go against the grain, so it should come as no surprise that my style and methods are neither popular nor easy to understand. But I manage money for others, and the world is not just populated with babbling but ultimately inconsequential journalists with no money to invest. So my wish is for investors in general to remain fools of randomness (so I can trade against them), yet that there remain a minority intelligent enough to value my methods and supply me with capital. I was fortunate to meet Donald Sussman who corresponds to such ideal investor; he helped me in the second stage of my career by backing the startup of Empirica, my trading firm, thus freeing me from the ills of Wall Street employment. My greatest risk is to become successful, as it would mean that my business is about to disappear; strange business, ours.

THREE

A MATHEMATICAL
MEDITATION ON HISTORY

On Monte Carlo simulation as a metaphor to understanding a sequence of random historical events. On randomness and artificial history. Age is beauty, almost always, and the new and the young are generally toxic. Send your history professor to an introductory class on sampling theory.

EUROPLAYBOY MATHEMATICS

The stereotype of a pure mathematician presents an anemic man with a shaggy beard and grimy and uncut fingernails silently laboring on a Spartan but disorganized desk. With thin shoulders and a pot belly, he sits in a grubby office, totally absorbed in his work, oblivious to the grunginess of his surroundings. He grew up in a communist regime and speaks English with an astringent and throaty Eastern European accent. When he eats, crumbs of food accumulate in his beard. With time he becomes more and more absorbed in his subject matter of pure theorems, reaching levels of ever increasing abstraction. The American public was recently exposed to one of these characters with the *unabomber*, the bearded and recluse mathematician who lived in a hut and took to murdering people who promoted modern technology. No journalist was capable of even coming close to describing the subject matter of his thesis, *Complex Boundaries*, as it has no intelligible equivalent – a complex number being an entirely abstract and imaginary number, the square root of minus one, an object that has no analog outside of the world of mathematics.

The name Monte Carlo conjures up the image of a suntanned urbane man of the Europlayboy variety entering a casino under a whiff of the Mediterranean breeze. He is an apt skier and tennis player, but also can hold his own in chess and bridge. He drives a gray sports car, dresses in a well ironed Italian handmade suit, and speaks carefully and smoothly about mundane, but real, matters, those a journalist can easily describe to the public in compact sentences. Inside the casino he astutely counts the cards, mastering the odds, and bets in a studied manner, his mind producing precise calculations of his optimal betting size. He could be James Bond's smarter lost brother.

Now when I think of Monte Carlo mathematics, I think of a happy combination of the two: the Monte Carlo man's realism without the shallowness combined with the mathematician's intuitions without the excessive abstraction. For indeed this branch of mathematics is of immense practical use – it does not present the same dryness commonly associated with mathematics. I became addicted to it the minute I became a trader. It shaped my thinking in most matters related to randomness. Most of the examples used in the book were created with my Monte Carlo generator, which I introduce in this chapter. Yet, it is far more a way of thinking than a computational method. Mathematics is principally a tool to meditate, rather than to compute.

THE TOOLS

The notion of alternative histories discussed in the last chapter can be extended considerably and subjected to all manner of technical refinement. This brings us to the tools used in my profession to toy with uncertainty. I will outline them next. Monte Carlo methods, in brief, consist in creating artificial history using the following concepts.

First, consider the sample path. The invisible histories have a scientific name, *alternative sample paths*, a name borrowed from the field of mathematics of probability called stochastic processes. The notion of path, as opposed to outcome, indicates that it is not a mere MBA-style scenario analysis, but the examination of a sequence of scenarios along the course of time. We are not just concerned at where a bird can end up tomorrow night, but rather at all the various places it can possibly visit during the time interval. We are not concerned with what the investor's worth would be in, say, a year, but rather of the heart-wrenching rides he may experience during that period. The word *sample* stresses that one sees only one realization among a collection of possible ones. Now a sample path can be both deterministic or random, which brings the next distinction.

A *random sample path*, also called a random run, is the mathematical name for such succession of virtual historical events, starting at a given date and ending at another, except that they are subjected to some varying level of uncertainty. However, the word random should not be mistaken for equiprobable (i.e. having the same probability). Some outcomes will give a higher probability than others. An example of a random sample path can be the body temperature of your explorer cousin during his latest bout with typhoid fever, measured hourly from the beginning to the end of his episode. It can also be a simulation of the price of your favorite technology stock, measured daily at the close of the market, over, say, one year. Starting at $100, in one scenario it can end up at $20 having seen a high of $220, in another it can end up at $145 having seen a low of $10. Another example is the evolution of your wealth during an evening at a casino. You start with $1000 in your pocket, and measure it every 15 minutes. In one sample path you have $2200 at midnight; in another you barely have $20 left for a cab fare.

Stochastic processes refer to the dynamics of events unfolding with the course of time. Stochastic is a fancy Greek name for random. This branch of probability concerns itself with the study of the evolution of successive random events – one could call it the mathematics of history. The key about a process is that it has time in it.

What is a Monte Carlo generator? Imagine that you can replicate a perfect roulette wheel in your attic without having recourse to a carpenter. Computer programs can be written to simulate just about anything. They are even better (and cheaper) than the roulette wheel built by your carpenter, as this may be inclined to favor one number more than others owing to a possible slant in its build or the floor of your attic. These are called the biases.

Monte Carlo simulations are closer to a toy than anything I have seen in my adult life. One can generate thousands, perhaps millions of random sample paths, and look at the prevalent characteristics of some of their features. The assistance of the computer is instrumental in such studies. The glamorous reference to Monte Carlo indicates the metaphor of simulating the random events in the manner of a virtual casino. One sets conditions believed to resemble the ones that prevail in reality, and launches a collection of simulations around possible events. With no mathematical literacy we can launch a Monte Carlo simulation of an 18-year-old Christian Lebanese playing successively Russian roulette for a given sum, and see how many of these attempts result in enrichment, or how long it takes on average before he hits the obituary. We can change the barrel to contain 500 holes, a matter that would decrease the probability of death, and see the results.

Monte Carlo simulation methods were pioneered in martial physics in the Los Alamos laboratory during the A bomb preparation. They became popular in financial mathematics in the 1980s, particularly in the theories of the random walk of asset prices. Clearly, we have to say that the example of Russian roulette does not need such apparatus, but many problems, particularly those resembling real-life situations, require the potency of a Monte Carlo simulator.

MONTE CARLO MATHEMATICS

It is a fact that "true" mathematicians do not like Monte Carlo methods. They believe that they rob us of the finesse and elegance of mathematics. They call it "brute force". For we can replace a large portion of mathematical knowledge with a Monte Carlo simulator (and other computational tricks). For instance, someone with no formal knowledge of geometry can compute the mysterious, almost mystical Pi. How? By drawing a circle inside of a square, and "shooting" random bullets into the picture (as in an arcade), specifying equal probabilities of hitting any point on the map (something called a uniform distribution). The ratio of bullets inside the circle divided by those inside and outside the circle will deliver a multiple of the mystical Pi, with possibly infinite precision. Clearly, this is not an efficient use of a computer as Pi can be computed analytically, that is, in a mathematical form, but the method can give some users more intuition about the subject matter than lines of equations. Some people's brains and intuitions are oriented in such a way that they are more capable of getting a point in such a manner (I count myself one of those). The computer might not be natural to our human brain; neither is mathematics.

I am not a "native" mathematician, that is, I am someone who does not speak mathematics as a native language, but someone who speaks it with a trace of a foreign accent. For I am not interested in mathematical properties *per se*, only in the application, while a mathematician would be interested in improving mathematics (via theorems and proofs). I proved incapable of concentrating on deciphering a single equation unless I was motivated by a real problem (with a modicum of greed); thus most of what I know comes from derivatives trading – options pushed me to study the math of probability. Many compulsive gamblers, who otherwise would be of middling intelligence, acquire remarkable card-counting skills thanks to their passionate greed.

Another analogy would be with grammar; mathematics is often tedious and insightless grammar. There are those who are interested in grammar for grammar's sake, and those interested in avoiding solecisms while writing documents. We are called "quants" – like physicists, we have more interest in the employment of the mathematical tool than in the tool itself. Mathematicians are born, never made. Physicists and quants too. I do not care about the "elegance" and "quality" of the mathematics I use so long as I can get the point right. I have recourse to Monte Carlo machines whenever I can. They can get the work done. They are also far more pedagogical, and I will use them in this book for the examples.

Indeed, probability is an introspective field of inquiry, as it affects more than one science, particularly the mother of all sciences; that of knowledge. It is impossible to assess the quality of the knowledge we are gathering without allowing a share of randomness in the manner it is obtained and cleaning the argument from the chance coincidence that could have seeped into its construction. In science, probability and information are treated in exactly the same manner. Literally every great thinker has dabbled with it, most of them obsessively. The two greatest minds to me, Einstein and Keynes, both started their intellectual journeys with it. Einstein wrote a major paper in 1905, in which he was almost the first to examine in probabilistic terms the succession of random events, namely the evolution of suspended particles in a stationary liquid. His theory on the theory of the Brownian movement can be used as the backbone of the random walk theories used in financial modeling. As for Keynes, to the literate person he is not the political economist that tweed-clad leftists love to quote, but the author of the magisterial, introspective, and potent *Treatise on Probability*. For before his venturing into the murky field of political economy, Keynes was a probabilist. He also had other interesting attributes (he blew up trading his account after experiencing excessive opulence – people's understanding of probability does not translate into their behavior).

The reader can guess that the next step from such probabilistic introspection is to get drawn into philosophy, particularly the branch of philosophy that concerns itself with knowledge, called epistemology or methodology, or philosophy of science, popularized by such persons as Karl Popper and George Soros. We will not get into the topic until later in the book.

Fun In My Attic

MAKING HISTORY

In the early 1990s, like many of my friends in quantitative finance, I became addicted to the various Monte Carlo engines, which I taught myself to build, thrilled to feel that I was generating history, a *Demiurgus*. It can be electrifying to generate virtual histories and watch the dispersion between the various results. Such dispersion is indicative of the degree of resistance to randomness. This is where I am convinced that I have been extremely lucky in my choice of career: one of the attractive aspects of my profession as a quantitative option trader is that

I have close to 95% of my day free to think, read, and research (or "reflect" in the gym, on ski slopes, or, more effectively, on a park bench). I also had the privilege of frequently "working" from my well-equipped attic.

The dividend of the computer revolution to us did not come in the flooding of self-perpetuating e-mail messages and access to chat rooms; it was in the sudden availability of fast processors capable of generating a million sample paths per minute. Recall that I never considered myself better than an unenthusiastic equation solver and was rarely capable of prowess in the matter – being better at setting up equations than solving them. Suddenly, my engine allowed me to solve with minimal effort the most intractable of equations. Few solutions became out of reach.

ZORGLUBS CROWDING THE ATTIC

My Monte Carlo engine took me on a few interesting adventures. While my colleagues were immersed in news stories, central bank announcements, earnings reports, economic forecasts, sports results and, not least, office politics, I started toying with it in fields bordering my home base of financial probability. A natural field of expansion for the amateur is evolutionary biology – the universality of its message and its application to markets are appealing. I started simulating populations of fast mutating animals called Zorglubs under climatic changes and witnessing the most unexpected of conclusions – some of the results are recycled in Chapter 5. My aim, as a pure amateur fleeing the boredom of business life, was merely to develop intuitions for these events – the sort of intuitions that amateurs build away from the overly detailed sophistication of the professional researcher. I also toyed with molecular biology, generating randomly occurring cancer cells and witnessing some surprising aspects to their evolution. Naturally the analogue to fabricating populations of Zorglubs was to simulate a population of "idiotic bull", "impetuous bear" and "cautious" traders under different market regimes, say booms and busts, and to examine their short-term and long-term survival. Under such a structure, "idiotic bull" traders who get rich from the rally would use the proceeds to buy more assets, driving prices higher, until their ultimate shellacking.

Bearish traders, though, rarely made it in the boom to get to the bust. My models showed almost nobody to really ultimately make money; bears dropped out like flies in the rally and bulls got ultimately slaughtered, as paper profits vanished when the music stopped. But there was one exception; some of those who traded options (I called them option buyers) had remarkable staying power and I wanted to be one of those. How? Because they could buy the insurance against blowup; they could get anxiety-free sleep at night, thanks to the knowledge that if their careers were threatened, it would not be owing to the outcome of a single day.

If the tone of this book seems steeped in the culture of Darwinism and evolutionary thinking, it does not come from any remotely formal training in the natural sciences, but from the evolutionary way of thinking taught by my Monte Carlo simulators.

I have to reckon that I outgrew the desire to generate random runs every time I want to explore an idea – but by dint of playing with a Monte Carlo engine for years I can no longer visualize a realized outcome without reference to the non-realized ones. I call that "summing under histories", borrowing the expression from the colorful physicist Richard Feynman who applied such methods to examine the dynamics of particles.

Using my Monte Carlo to do and redo history reminded me of the experimental novels (the so-called *new novels*) by such writers as Alain Robbe-Grillet, popular in the 1960s and 1970s. There the same chapter would be written and revised, the writer each time changing the plot like a new sample path. Somehow the author was freed from the past situation he helped create and allowed himself the indulgence to change the plot retroactively.

DENIGRATION OF HISTORY

One more word on history seen from a Monte Carlo perspective. The wisdom of such classical stories as Solon prods me to spend even more time in the company of the classical historians, even if the stories, like Solon's warning, have benefited from the patina of time. However, this goes against the grain: learning from history does not come naturally to us humans, a fact that is so visible in the endless repetitions of identically configured booms and busts in modern markets. By history I refer to the anecdotes, not the historical theorizing, the grand-scale historicism that aims to interpret events with theories based on uncovering some laws in the evolution of history – the sort of Hegelianism and pseudoscientific historicism leading to such calls as the end of history (it is pseudoscientific because it draws theories from past events without allowing for the fact that such combinations of events might have arisen from randomness; it is mostly pseudoscientific because there is no way to verify the claims in a controlled experiment[2]). It is merely at the level of my desired sensibility, affecting the way I would wish to think by reference to past events, by being able to better steal the ideas of others and leverage them, correct the mental defect that seems to block my ability to learn from others. It is the respect of the elders that I would like to develop, reinforcing the awe I instinctively feel for people with gray hair, but that has eroded in my life as a trader where age and success are somewhat divorced. Indeed, I have two ways of learning from history: from the past by reading the elders, and from the future thanks to my Monte Carlo toy.

THE STOVE IS HOT

As I mentioned above, it is not natural for us to learn from history. We have enough clues to believe that our genetic endowment as *homo erectus* does not favor transfers of experience. It is a platitude that children learn only from their own mistakes; they will cease to touch a burning stove only when they are themselves burned; no possible warning by others can lead to developing the smallest form of cautiousness. Adults, too, suffer from such a condition. This point has been examined by behavioral economics pioneers Daniel Kahneman and Amos Tversky with regards to the choices people make in selecting risky medical treatments – I myself have seen it in my being extremely lax in the area of detection and prevention (i.e., I refuse to derive my risks from the probabilities computed on others, feeling that I am somewhat special) yet extremely aggressive in the treatment of medical conditions (I overreact when I am burned), which is not coherent with rational behavior under uncertainty. This congenital denigration of the experience of others is not limited to children or to people like myself; it affects business decision makers and investors on a grand scale.

All of my colleagues whom I have known to denigrate history blew up spectacularly – and I have yet to encounter some such person who has not blown up. But the truly interesting point lies in the remarkable similarities in their approaches. I have noticed plenty of analogies between those who blew up in the stock market crash of 1987, those who blew up in the Japan meltdown of 1990, those who blew up in the bond market débâcle of 1994, those who blew up in Russia in 1998, and those who blew up buying Nasdaq stocks in 2000. They all made claims to the effect that "these times are different" or that "their market was different", and offered seemingly well constructed intellectual arguments (of an economic nature) to justify their claims; they were unable to accept that the experience of others was out there, in the open, freely available to all, with books detailing crashes in every bookstore. Aside from these generalized systemic blow ups, I have seen hundreds of option traders forced to leave the business after blowing up in a stupid manner, in spite of warnings by the veterans, similar to a child's touching the stove. This I find to resemble my own personal attitude with respect to the detection and prevention of the variety of ailments I may be subjected to. Every man believes himself to be quite different, a matter that amplifies the "why me?" shock upon a diagnosis.

We can discuss this point from different angles. Experts call one manifestation of such denigration of history *historical determinism*. In a nutshell we think that we would know when history is made; we believe that people who, say, witnessed the stock market crash of 1929 knew then that they lived an acute historical event, and that, should these events repeat themselves, they would know about such facts. Life for us is made to resemble an adventure movie, as we know ahead of time that something big is about to happen. It is hard to imagine that people who witnessed history did not know at the time how important the moment was. Somehow all respect we may have for history does not translate well into our treatment of the present.

MY SOLON

I have another reason to be obsessed with Solon's warning. I hark back to the very same strip of land in the Eastern Mediterranean where the story took place. My ancestors experienced bouts of extreme opulence and embarrassing penury over the course of a single generation, with abrupt regressions that people around me who have the memory of steady and linear betterment, do not think feasible (at least not at the time of writing). Those around me either have (so far) had few family setbacks (except for the great depression) or, more generally, are not suffused with enough sense of history to reflect backward. For people of my background, Eastern Mediterranean Greek-Orthodox and invaded Eastern Roman citizens, it was as if our soul had been wired with the remembrance of that sad April day *circa* 500 years ago when Constantinople, under the invading Turks, fell out of history, leaving us the lost subjects of a dead empire, very prosperous minorities in an Islamic world – but with an extremely fragile wealth. Moreover, I vividly remember the image of my own dignified grandfather, a former deputy prime minister and son of a deputy prime minister (whom I never saw without a suit), residing in a nondescript apartment in Athens, his estate having been blown up during the Lebanese civil war. Incidentally, having experienced the ravages of war, I find undignified impoverishment far harsher than physical danger (somehow dying in full dignity appears to me far preferable to living a janitorial life, which is one of the reasons I dislike financial risks far more than physical ones). I am certain that Croesus worried more about the loss of his Kingdom than the perils to his life.

There is an important and non-trivial aspect of historical thinking, perhaps more applicable to the markets than anything else: unlike many "hard" sciences, history cannot lend itself to experimentation. But somehow, overall, history is potent enough to deliver, on time, in the medium to long run, most of the possible scenarios, burying the bad guy. Bad trades catch up with you, it is frequently said in the markets. Mathematicians of probability give that a fancy name: *ergodicity*. It means, roughly, that (under certain conditions), very long sample paths would end up resembling each other. The properties of a very, very long sample path would be similar to the Monte Carlo properties of an average of shorter ones. The janitor in Chapter 1 who won the lottery, if he lived 1000 years, cannot be expected to win more lotteries. Those who were unlucky in life in spite of their skills would eventually rise. The lucky fool might have benefited from some luck in life; over the longer run he would slowly converge to the state of a less-lucky idiot. Each one would revert to his long-term properties.

Distilled Thinking on Your PalmPilot

BREAKING NEWS

The journalist, my *bête noire*, entered this book with George Will dealing with random outcomes. In the next step I will show how my Monte Carlo toy taught me to favor distilled thinking, by which I mean the thinking based on information around us that is stripped of meaningless but diverting clutter. For the difference between noise and information, the topic of this book (noise has more randomness) has an analog: that between journalism and history. To be competent, a journalist should view matters like a historian, and play down the value of the information he is providing, such as by saying: "today the market went up, but this information is not too relevant as it emanates mostly from noise". He would certainly lose his job by trivializing the value of the information in his hands. Not only is it difficult for the journalist to think more like a historian, but it is alas the historian who is becoming more like the journalist.

For an idea, age is beauty (it is premature to discuss the mathematics of the point). The applicability of Solon's warning to a life in randomness, in contrast with the exact opposite message delivered by the prevailing media-soaked culture, reinforces my instinct to value distilled thought over newer thinking, regardless of its apparent sophistication – another reason to accumulate the hoary volumes by my bedside (I confess that the only news items I currently read are the far more interesting upscale social gossip stories found in *Tatler*, *Paris Match* and *Vanity Fair* – in addition to *The Economist*). Aside from the decorum of ancient thought as opposed to the coarseness of fresh ink, I spent some time phrasing the idea in the mathematics of evolutionary arguments and conditional probability. For an idea to have survived so long across so many cycles is indicative of its relative fitness. Noise, at least *some* noise, was filtered out. Mathematically, progress means that some new information is better than past information, not that the average of new information will supplant past information, which means that it is optimal for someone, when in doubt, to systematically reject the new idea, information, or method. Clearly and shockingly, always. Why?

The argument in favor of "new things" and even more "new new things" goes as follows: look at the dramatic changes that have been brought about by the arrival of new technologies, such as the automobile, the airplane, the telephone, and the personal computer. Middlebrow inference (inference stripped of probabilistic thinking) would lead one to believe that all new technologies and inventions would likewise revolutionize our lives. But the answer is not so obvious: here we only see and count the winners, to the exclusion of the losers (it is like saying that actors and writers are rich, ignoring the fact that actors are largely waiters – and lucky to be ones for the less comely writers usually serve French fries at McDonald's). Losers? The Saturday newspaper lists dozens of new patents of such items that can revolutionize our lives. People tend to infer that because *some* inventions have revolutionized our lives that inventions are good to endorse and we should favor the new over the old. I hold the opposite view. The opportunity cost of missing a "new new thing" like the airplane and the automobile is minuscule compared to the toxicity of all the garbage one has to go through to get to these jewels (assuming these have brought some improvement to our lives, which I frequently doubt).

Now the exact same argument applies to information. The problem with information is not that it is diverting and generally useless, but that it is toxic. We will examine the dubious value of the highly frequent news with a more technical discussion of signal filtering and observation frequency further down. I will say here that such respect for the time honored provides arguments to rule out any commerce with the babbling modern journalist and implies a minimal exposure to the media as a guiding principle for someone involved in decision-making under uncertainty. If there is anything better than noise in the mass of "urgent" news pounding us, it would be like a needle in a haystack. People do not realize that the media is paid to get your attention. For a journalist, silence rarely surpasses any word.

On the rare occasions when I boarded the 6:42 train to New York I observed with amazement the hordes of depressed business commuters (who seemed to have preferred to be elsewhere) studiously buried in the *Wall Street Journal*, apprised of the minutiae of companies that, at the time of writing, are probably out of business. Indeed it is difficult to ascertain whether they seem depressed because they are reading the newspaper, or if depressive people tend to read the newspaper, or if people who are living outside their genetic habitat both read the newspaper and look sleepy and depressed. But while early on in my career such focus on noise would have offended me intellectually, as I would have deemed such information as too statistically insignificant for the derivation of any meaningful conclusion, I currently look at it with delight. I am happy to see such mass-scale idiotic decision-making, prone to overreaction in their post-perusal investment orders – in other words I currently see in the fact that people read such material an insurance for my continuing in the entertaining business of option trading against the fools of randomness.

SHILLER REDUX

Much of the thinking about the negative value of information on society in general was sparked by Robert Shiller. Not just in financial markets; but overall his 1981 paper may be the first mathematically formulated introspection on the manner society in general handles information. Shiller made his mark with his 1981 paper on the volatility of markets, where he determined that, if a stock price is the estimated value of "something" (say the discounted cash flows from a corporation), then market prices are way too volatile in relation to tangible manifestations of that "something" (he used dividends as proxy). Prices swing more than the fundamentals they are supposed to reflect, they visibly overreact by being too high at times (when their price overshoots the good news or when they go up without any marked reason) or too low at others. The volatility differential between prices and information meant that something about "rational expectation" did not work. (Prices did not rationally reflect the long-term value of securities by overshooting in either direction.) Markets had to be wrong. Shiller then pronounced markets to be not as efficient as established by financial theory (efficient markets meant, in a nutshell, that prices should adapt to all available information in such a way as to be totally unpredictable to us humans and prevent people from deriving profits). This conclusion set off calls by the religious orders of high finance for the destruction of the infidel who committed such apostasy. Interestingly, and by some strange coincidence, it is that very same Shiller that was trounced by George Will only one chapter ago.

The principal criticism against Shiller came from Robert C. Merton. The attacks were purely on methodological grounds (Shiller's analysis was extremely rough; for instance, his using dividends in place of earnings was rather weak). Merton was also defending the official financial theory position that markets needed to be efficient and could not possibly deliver opportunities on a silver plate. Yet the same Robert C. Merton later introduced himself as the "founding partner" of a hedge fund that aimed at taking advantage of market inefficiencies. Setting aside the fact that Merton's hedge fund blew up rather spectacularly from the *black swan problem* (with characteristic denial), his "founding" such a hedge fund requires, by implication, that he agrees with Shiller about the inefficiency of the market. The defender of the dogmas of modern finance and efficient markets started a fund that took advantage of market inefficiencies! It is as if the Pope converted to Islam.

Things are not getting any better these days. At the time of writing, news providers are offering all manner of updates, "breaking news" that can be delivered electronically in a wireless manner. The ratio of undistilled information to distilled is rising, saturating markets. The elder's messages need not be delivered to you as imminent news.

This does not mean that all journalists are fooled by randomness noise providers: there are hordes of thoughtful journalists in the business (I would suggest London's Anatole Kaletsky and New York's Jim Grant and Alan Abelson as the underrated representatives of such a class among financial journalists; Gary Stix among scientific journalists); it is just that prominent media journalism is a thoughtless process of providing the noise that can capture people's attention and there exists no mechanism for separating the two. As a matter of fact smart journalists are often penalized. Like the lawyer in Chapter 11 who does not care about the truth, but about arguments that can sway a jury whose intellectual defects he knows intimately, journalism goes to what can capture our attention, with adequate sound-bites. Again my scholarly friends would wonder why I am getting emotional stating the obvious things about the journalists; the problem with my profession is that we depend on them for what information we need to obtain.

GERONTOCRACY

A preference for distilled thinking implies favoring old investors and traders, that is investors who have been exposed to markets the longest, a matter that is counter to the common Wall Street practice of preferring those that have been the most profitable, and preferring the younger whenever possible. I toyed with Monte Carlo simulations of heterogeneous populations of traders under a variety of regimes (closely resembling historical ones), and found a significant advantage in selecting aged traders, using, as a selection criterion their cumulative years of experience rather than their absolute success (conditional on their having survived without blowing up). "Survival of the fittest", a term so hackneyed in the investment media, does not seem to be properly understood: under regime switching, as we will see in Chapter 5, it will be unclear who is actually the fittest, and those who will survive are not necessarily those who appear to be the fittest. Curiously, it will be the oldest, simply because older people have been exposed longer to the rare event and can be, convincingly, more resistant to it. I was amused to discover a similar evolutionary argument in mate selection that considers that women prefer (on balance) to mate with healthy older men over healthy younger ones, everything else being equal, as the former provide some evidence of better genes. Gray hair signals an enhanced ability to survive – conditional on having reached the gray hair stage, he is likely to be more resistant to the vagaries of life. Curiously, life insurers in renaissance Italy reached the same conclusion, by charging the same insurance for a man in his 20s as they did for a man in his 50s, a sign that they had the same life expectation; once a man crossed the 40-year mark, he had shown that very few ailments could harm him. We now proceed to a mathematical rephrasing of these arguments.

Philostratus in Monte Carlo: On the Difference Between Noise and Information

The wise man listens to meaning, the fool only gets the noise. The modern Greek poet C. P. Cavafy wrote a piece in 1915 after Philostratus' adage: *For the gods perceive things in the future, ordinary people things in the present, but the wise perceive things about to happen.* Cavafy wrote:

> *in their intense meditation the hidden sound of things approaching reaches them and they listen reverently while in the street outside the people hear nothing at all.*

I thought hard and long on how to explain with as little mathematics as possible the difference between noise and meaning, and how to show why the time scale is important in judging an historical event. The Monte Carlo simulator can provide us with such an intuition. We will start with an example borrowed from the investment world (that is my profession), as it can be explained rather easily, but the concept can be used in any application.

Let us manufacture a happily retired dentist, living in a pleasant sunny town. We know *a priori* that he is an excellent investor, and that he will be expected to earn a return of 15% in excess of Treasury bills, with a 10% error rate per annum (what we call volatility). It means that out of 100 sample paths, we expect close to 68 of them to fall within a band of plus and minus 10% around the 15% excess return, i.e. between 5% and 25% (to be technical; the bell-shaped normal distribution has 68% of all observations falling between −1 and 1 standard deviations). It also means that 95 sample paths would fall between −5% and 35%.

Clearly, we are dealing with a very optimistic situation. The dentist builds for himself a nice trading desk in his attic, aiming to spend every business day there watching the market, while sipping decaffeinated cappuccino. He has an adventurous temperament, so he finds this activity more attractive than drilling the teeth of reluctant old little Park Avenue ladies.

He subscribes to a web-based service that supplies him with continuous prices, now to be obtained for a fraction of what he pays for his coffee. He puts his inventory of securities in his spreadsheet and can thus instantaneously monitor the value of his speculative portfolio. We are living in the era called that of connectivity.

A 15% return with a 10% volatility (or uncertainty) per annum translates into a 93% probability of making money in any given year. But seen at a narrow time scale, this translates into a mere 50.02% probability of making money over any given second as shown in Table 3.1. Over the very narrow time increment, the observation will reveal close to nothing. Yet the dentist's heart will not tell him that. Being emotional, he feels a pang with every loss, as it shows in red on his screen. He feels some pleasure when the performance is positive, but not in equivalent amount as the pain experienced when the performance is negative.

At the end of every day the dentist will be emotionally drained. A minute-by-minute examination of his performance means that each day (assuming eight hours per day) he will have 241 pleasurable minutes against 239 unpleasurable ones. These amount to 60,688 and 60,271, respectively, per year. Now realize that if the unpleasurable minute is

Table 3.1 Probability of making money at different scales.

Scale	Probability
1 year	93%
1 quarter	77%
1 month	67%
1 day	54%
1 hour	51.3%
1 minute	50.17%
1 second	50.02%

worse in reverse pleasure than the pleasurable minute is in pleasure terms, then the dentist incurs a large deficit when examining his performance at a high frequency.

Consider the situation where the dentist examines his portfolio only upon receiving the monthly account from the brokerage house. As 67% of his months will be positive, he incurs only four pangs of pain per annum and eight uplifting experiences. This is the same dentist following the same strategy. Now consider the dentist looking at his performance only every year. Over the next 20 years that he is expected to live, he will experience 19 pleasant surprises for every unpleasant one!

This scaling property of randomness is generally misunderstood, even by professionals. I have seen Ph.D.s argue over a performance observed in a narrow time scale (meaningless by any standard). Before additional dumping on the journalist, more observations seem in order.

Viewing it from another angle, if we take the ratio of noise to what we call nonnoise (i.e., left column/right column), which we have the privilege here of examining quantitatively, then we have the following. Over one year we observe roughly 0.7 parts noise for every one part performance. Over one month, we observe roughly 2.32 parts noise for every one part performance. Over one hour, 30 parts noise for every one part performance, and over one second, 1796 parts noise for every one part performance.

A few conclusions:

1. Over a short time increment, one observes the variability of the portfolio, not the returns. In other words, one sees the variance, little else. I always remind myself that what one observes is at best a combination of variance and returns, not just returns.
2. Our emotions are not designed to understand the point. The dentist did better when he dealt with monthly statements rather than infrequent ones. Perhaps it would be even better for him if he limited himself to yearly statements.
3. When I see an investor monitoring his portfolio with live prices on his cellular telephone or his PalmPilot, I smile and smile.

Finally I reckon that I am not immune to such an emotional defect. But I deal with it by having no access to information, except in rare circumstances. Again, I prefer to read poetry. If an event is important enough, it will find its way to my ears. I will return to this point in time.

The same methodology can explain why the news (the high scale) is full of noise and why history (the low scale) is largely stripped of it (though fraught with interpretation problems). This explains why I prefer not to read the newspaper (outside of the obituary), why I never chitchat about markets, and, when in a trading room, I frequent the mathematicians and the secretaries, not the traders. It explains why it is better to read *The Economist* on Saturdays than the *Wall Street Journal* every morning (from the standpoint of frequency, aside from the massive gap in intellectual class between the two publications).

Finally, this explains why people who look too closely at randomness burn out, their emotions drained by the series of pangs they experience. Regardless of what people claim, a negative pang is not offset by a positive one (some behavioral economists estimate the negative effect to be up to 2.5 the magnitude of a positive one); it will lead to an emotional deficit.

Some so-called wise and rational persons often blame me for "ignoring" possible valuable information in the daily newspaper and refusing to discount the details of the noise as "short-term events". Some of my employers have blamed me for living on a different planet.

My problem is that I am not rational and I am extremely prone to drown in randomness and to incur emotional torture. I am aware of my need to ruminate on park benches and in cafés away from information, but I can only do so if I am somewhat deprived of it. My sole advantage in life is that I know some of my weaknesses, mostly that I am incapable of taming my emotions facing news and incapable of seeing a performance with a clear head. Silence is far better. More on that in Part III.

FOUR

✛

RANDOMNESS, NONSENSE, AND THE SCIENTIFIC INTELLECTUAL

On extending the Monte Carlo generator to produce artificial thinking and compare it with rigorous non-random constructs. The science wars enter the business world. Why the aesthete in me loves to be fooled by randomness.

Randomness and the Verb

Our Monte Carlo engine can take us into more literary territory. Increasingly, a distinction is being made between the scientific intellectual and the literary intellectual – culminating with what is called the "science wars", plotting factions of literate non-scientists against no less literate scientists. The distinction between the two approaches originated in Vienna in the 1930s, with a collection of physicists who decided that the large gains in science were becoming significant enough to make claims on the field known to belong to the humanities. In their view, literary thinking could conceal plenty of well-sounding nonsense. They wanted to strip thinking from rhetoric (except in literature and poetry where it properly belonged).

The way they introduced rigor into intellectual life is by declaring that a statement could fall only into two categories: *deductive*, like "2 + 2 = 4", i.e., incontrovertibly flowing from a precisely defined axiomatic framework (here the rules of arithmetic), or *inductive*, i.e., verifiable in some manner (experience, statistics, etc.), like "it rains in Spain" or "New Yorkers are generally rude". Anything else was plain unadulterated hogwash (music could be a far better replacement to metaphysics). Needless to say that inductive statements may turn out to be difficult, even impossible, to verify, as we will see with the black swan problem – and empiricism can be worse than any other form of hogwash when it gives someone confidence (it will take me a few chapters to drill the point). However, it was a good start to make intellectuals responsible for providing some form of evidence for their statements. This Vienna Circle was at the origin of the development of the ideas of Wittgenstein, Popper, Carnap, and flocks of others. Whatever merit their original ideas may have, the impact on both philosophy and the practice of science has been significant. Some of their impact on non-philosophical intellectual life is starting to develop, albeit considerably more slowly.

One conceivable way to discriminate between a scientific intellectual and a literary intellectual is by considering that a scientific intellectual can usually recognize the writing of another but that the literary intellectual would not be able to tell the difference between lines jotted down by a scientist and those by a glib non-scientist. This is even more apparent when the literary intellectual starts using scientific buzzwords, like "uncertainty principle", "Gödel's theorem", "parallel universe", or "relativity" either out of context or, as often, in exact opposition to the scientific meaning. I suggest reading the hilarious *Fashionable Nonsense* by Alan Sokal for an illustration of such practice (I was laughing so loudly and so frequently while reading it on a plane that other passengers kept whispering things about me). By dumping the kitchen sink of scientific references in a paper, one can make another literary intellectual believe that one's material has the stamp of science. Clearly, to a scientist, science lies in the rigor of the inference, not in random references to such grandiose concepts as general relativity or quantum indeterminacy. Such rigor can be spelled out in plain English. Science is method and rigor; it can be identified in the simplest of prose writing. For instance, what struck me while reading Richard Dawkins' *Selfish Gene*[3] is that, although the text does not exhibit a single equation, it seems as if it were translated from the language of mathematics. Yet it is artistic prose.

REVERSE TURING TEST

Randomness can be of considerable help with the matter. For there is another, far more entertaining way to make the distinction between the babbler and the thinker. You can sometimes replicate something that can be mistaken for a literary discourse with a Monte Carlo generator but it is not possible randomly to construct a scientific one. Rhetoric can be constructed randomly, but not genuine scientific knowledge. This is the application of *Turing's test* of artificial intelligence, except in reverse. What is the Turing test? The brilliant British mathematician, eccentric, and computer pioneer Alan Turing came up with the following test: a computer can be said to be intelligent if it can (on average) fool a human into mistaking it for another human. The converse should be true. A human can be said to be unintelligent if we can replicate his speech by a computer, which we know is unintelligent, and fool a human into believing that it was written by a human. Can one produce a piece of work that can be largely mistaken for Derrida entirely randomly?

The answer seems to be yes. Aside from the hoax by Alan Sokal (the same of the hilarious book a few lines ago) who managed to produce nonsense and get it published by some prominent journal,[4] there are Monte Carlo generators designed to structure such texts and write entire papers. Fed with "postmodernist" texts, they can randomize phrases under a method called recursive grammar, and produce grammatically sound but entirely meaningless sentences that sound like Jacques Derrida, Camille Paglia, and such a crowd. Owing to the fuzziness of his thought, the literary intellectual can be fooled by randomness.

At the Monash University program in Australia featuring the Dada Engine built by Andrew C. Bulha,[5] I toyed with the engine and generated a few papers containing the following sentences:

However, the main theme of the works of Rushdie is not theory, as the dialectic paradigm of reality suggests, but pretheory. The premise of the neosemanticist paradigm of discourse implies that sexual identity, ironically, has significance.

Many narratives concerning the role of the writer as observer may be revealed. It could be said that if cultural narrative holds, we have to choose between the dialectic paradigm of narrative and neo-conceptual Marxism. Sartre's analysis of cultural narrative holds that society, paradoxically, has objective value.

Thus, the premise of the neodialectic paradigm of expression implies that consciousness may be used to reinforce hierarchy, but only if reality is distinct from consciousness; if that is not the case, we can assume that language has intrinsic meaning.

Some business speeches belong to this category in their own right, except that they are less elegant and draw on a different type of vocabulary than the literary ones. We can randomly construct a speech imitating that of your chief executive officer to insure whether what he is saying has value, or if it is merely dressed-up nonsense from someone who was lucky to be put there. How? You select randomly five phrases below, then connect them by adding the minimum required to construct a grammatically sound speech.

We look after our customer's interests/the road ahead/our assets are our people/creation of shareholder value/our vision/our expertise lies in/we provide interactive solutions/we position ourselves in this market/how to serve our customers better/short term pain for long term gain/we will be rewarded in the long run/we play from our strength and improve our weaknesses/courage and determination will prevail/we are committed to innovation and technology/a happy employee is a productive employee/commitment to excellence/strategic plan/our work ethics.

If this bears too close a resemblance to the speech you just heard from the boss of your company, then I suggest looking for a new job.

THE FATHER OF ALL PSEUDOTHINKERS

It is hard to resist discussion of artificial history without a comment on the father of all pseudothinkers, Hegel. Hegel writes a jargon that is meaningless outside of a chic Left-Bank Parisian café or the humanities department of some university extremely well insulated from the real world. I suggest this passage from the German "philosopher" (this passage was detected, translated and reviled by Karl Popper):

> *Sound is the change in the specific condition of segregation of the material parts, and in the negation of this condition; merely an abstract or an ideal ideality, as it were, of that specification. But this change, accordingly, is itself immediately the negation of the material specific subsistence; which is, therefore, real ideality of specific gravity and cohesion, i.e. – heat. The heating up of sounding bodies, just as of beaten and or rubbed ones, is the appearance of heat, originating conceptually together with sound.*

Even a Monte Carlo engine could not sound as random as the great philosophical master thinker (it would take plenty of sample runs to get the mixture of *heat* and *sound*). People call that philosophy and frequently finance it with taxpayer subsidies! Now consider that Hegelian thinking is generally linked to a "scientific" approach to history; it has produced such results as Marxist regimes and even a branch called "neo-Hegelian" thinking. These "thinkers" should be given an undergraduate-level class on statistical sampling theory prior to their release in the open world.

Monte Carlo Poetry

There are instances where I like to be fooled by randomness. My allergy to nonsense and verbiage dissipates when it comes to art and poetry. On the one hand, I try to define myself and behave officially as a no-nonsense hyper-realist ferreting out the role of chance; on the other, I have no qualms indulging in all manner of personal superstitions. Where do I draw the line? The answer is aesthetics. Some aesthetic forms appeal to something genetic in us, whether or not they originate in random associations or plain hallucination. Something in our human genes is deeply moved by the fuzziness and ambiguity of language; then why fight it?

The poetry and language-lover in me was initially depressed by the account of the *Exquisite Cadavers* poetic exercise where interesting and poetic sentences are randomly constructed. By throwing enough words together, some unusual and magical-sounding metaphor is bound to emerge according to the laws of combinatorics. Yet one cannot deny that some of these poems are of ravishing beauty. Who cares about their origin if they manage to please our aesthetic senses?

The story of the *Exquisite Cadavers* is as follows. In the aftermath of the First World War, a collection of surrealist poets, which included André Breton, their pope, Paul Eluard, and others got together in cafés and tried the following exercise (modern literary critics attribute the exercise to the depressed mood after the war and the need to escape reality). On a folded piece of paper, in turn, each one of them would write a predetermined part of a sentence, not knowing the other's choice. The first would pick an adjective, the second a noun, the third a verb, the fourth an adjective, and the fifth a noun. The first publicized exercise of such random (and collective) arrangement produced the following poetic sentence:

The exquisite cadavers shall drink the new wine

(*Les cadavres exquis boiront le vin nouveau*). Impressive? It sounds even more poetic in the native French. Quite impressive poetry was produced in such a manner, sometimes with the aid of a computer. But poetry has never been truly taken seriously outside of the beauty of its associations, whether they have been produced by the random ranting of one or more disorganized brains, or the more elaborate constructions of one conscious creator.

Now regardless of whether the poetry was obtained by a Monte Carlo engine or sung by a blind man in Asia Minor, language is potent in bringing pleasure and solace. Testing its intellectual validity by translating it into simple logical arguments would rob it of a varying degree of its potency, sometimes excessively; nothing can be more bland than translated poetry. A convincing argument of the role of language is the existence of surviving holy languages, uncorrupted by the no-nonsense tests of daily use. Semitic religions, that is Judaism, Islam, and original Christianity understood the point; keep a language away from the rationalization of daily use and avoid the corruption of the vernacular. Four decades ago, the Catholic church translated the services and liturgies from Latin to the local vernaculars; it can be argued that this caused a drop in religious beliefs. Suddenly religion subjected itself to being judged by intellectual and scientific, without the aesthetic, standards. The Greek Orthodox church made the lucky mistake, upon translating some of its prayers from Church-Greek into the Semitic-based vernacular spoken by the Grecosyrians of the Antioch region (Southern Turkey and Northern Syria), of choosing classical Arabic, an entirely dead language. My folks are thus lucky to pray in a mixture of dead *Koiné* (Church Greek) and no less dead Koranic Arabic.

What does this point have to do with a book on randomness? Our genes dictate a need for *péché mignon*. Even the economists, who usually find abstruse ways completely to escape reality, are starting to understand that what makes us tick is not necessarily the calculating accountant in us. We do not need to be rational and scientific when it comes to the details of our daily life – only in those that can harm us and threaten our survival. Modern life seems to invite us to do the exact opposite; become extremely realistic and intellectual when it comes to such matters as religion and personal behavior, yet as irrational as possible when it comes to markets and matters ruled by randomness. I have encountered colleagues, "rational" no-nonsense people, who do not understand why I cherish the poetry of Baudelaire or obscure (and often impenetrable) writers like Elias Canetti, Borges, or Saint-John Perse. Yet they get sucked into listening to the "analyses" of a television "guru", or into buying the stock of a company they know absolutely nothing about, based on tips by neighbors who drive expensive cars. The Vienna Circle, in their dumping on Hegel-style verbiage-based philosophy, explained that, from a scientific standpoint, it was plain garbage, and, from an artistic point of view, it was inferior to music. I have to say that I find Baudelaire far more pleasant to frequent than CNN newscasters or listening to George Will.

There is a Yiddish saying: *If I am going to be forced to eat pork, it better be of the best kind.* If I am going to be fooled by randomness, it better be of the beautiful (and harmless) kind. This point will be made again in Part III.

FIVE

SURVIVAL OF THE LEAST FIT - CAN EVOLUTION BE FOOLED BY RANDOMNESS?

A case study on two rare events. On rare events and evolution. How "Darwinism" and evolution are concepts that are misunderstood in the non-biological world. Life is not continuous. How evolution will be fooled by randomness. A preparation to the problem of induction.

Carlos the Emerging Markets Wizard

I used to meet Carlos at a variety of New York parties, where he would show up impeccably dressed, though a bit shy with the ladies. I used to regularly pounce on him and try to pick his brains about what he did for a living, namely buying or selling emerging market bonds. A nice gentleman, he complied with my requests, but tensed up; for him speaking English, in spite of his fluency, seemed to require some expenditure of physical effort that made him contract his head and neck muscles (some people are not made to speak foreign languages). What are emerging market bonds? "Emerging market" is the politically correct euphemism to define a country that is not very developed (as a skeptic, I do not impart to their "emergence" such linguistic certainty). The bonds are financial instruments issued by these foreign governments, mostly Russia, Mexico, Brazil, Argentina, and Turkey. These bonds traded for pennies when these governments were not doing well. Suddenly investors rushed into these markets in the early 1990s and pushed the envelope further and further by acquiring increasingly more exotic securities. All these countries were building hotels where United States cable news channels were available, with health clubs equipped with treadmills and large-screen television sets that made them join the global village. They all had access to the same gurus and financial entertainers. Bankers would come to invest in their bonds and the countries would use the proceeds to build nicer hotels so more investors would visit. At some point these bonds became the vogue and went from pennies to dollars; those who knew the slightest thing about them accumulated vast fortunes.

Carlos supposedly comes from a patrician Latin-American family that was heavily impoverished by the economic troubles of the 1980s, but, again, I have rarely run into anyone from a ravaged country whose family did not at some juncture own an entire province or, say, supply the Russian Czar with sets of dominoes. After brilliant undergraduate studies, he went to Harvard to pursue a Ph.D. in economics, as it was the sort of thing Latin-American patricians had gotten into the habit of doing at the time (with a view to saving their economies from the evils of non-Ph.D. hands). He was a good student but could not find a decent thesis topic for his dissertation. Nor did he gain the respect of his thesis advisor, who found him unimaginative. Carlos settled for a Master's degree and a Wall Street career.

The nascent emerging market desk of a New York bank hired Carlos in 1992. He had the right ingredients for success; he knew where on the map to find the countries that issued "Brady bonds", dollar-denominated debt instruments issued by Less Developed Countries. He knew what Gross Domestic Product meant. He looked serious, brainy and well spoken, in spite of his heavy Spanish accent. He was the kind of person banks felt comfortable putting in front of their customers. What a contrast with the other traders who lacked polish!

Carlos got there right in time to see things happening in that market. When he joined the bank, the market for emerging market debt instruments was small and traders were located in undesirable parts of trading floors. But the activity rapidly became a large, and growing, part of the bank's revenues.

He was generic among this community of emerging market traders; they are a collection of cosmopolitan patricians from across the emerging market world that remind me of the international coffee hour at the Wharton School. I find it odd that rarely does a person specialize in the market of his or her birthplace. Mexicans based in London trade Russian securities, Iranians and Greeks specialize in Brazilian bonds, and Argentines trade Turkish securities. Unlike my experience with real traders, they are generally urbane, dress well, collect art, but are non-intellectual. They seem too conformist to be true traders. They are mostly between 30 and 40, owing to the youth of their market. You can expect many of them to hold season tickets to the Metropolitan Opera. True traders, I believe, dress sloppily, are often ugly and exhibit the intellectual curiosity of someone who would be more interested in the information-revealing contents of the garbage can than the Cézanne painting on the wall.

Carlos thrived as a trader-economist. He had a large network of friends in the various Latin-American countries and knew exactly what took place there. He bought bonds that he found attractive, either because they paid him a good rate of interest, or because he believed that they would become more in demand in the future, therefore appreciating in price. It would be perhaps erroneous to call him a *trader*. A trader buys and sells (he may sell what he does not own and buy it back later, hopefully making a profit in a decline; this is called "shorting"). Carlos just bought – and he bought in size. He believed that he was paid a good risk premium to hold these bonds because there was economic value in lending to these countries. Shorting, in his opinion, made no economic sense.

Within the bank Carlos was the emerging markets reference. He could produce the latest economic figures at the drop of a hat. He had frequent lunches with the chairman. In his opinion, trading was economics, little else. It had worked so well for him. He got promotion after promotion, until he became the head trader of the emerging market desk at the institution. Starting in 1995, Carlos did exponentially well in his new function, getting an expansion of his capital on a steady basis (i.e., the bank allocated a larger portion of its funds to his operation) – so fast that he was incapable of using up the new risk limits.

THE GOOD YEARS

The reason Carlos had good years was not just because he bought emerging market bonds and their value went up over the period. It was mostly because he also bought dips. He accumulated when prices experienced a momentary panic. The year 1997 would have been a bad year had he not added to his position after the dip in October that accompanied the false stock market crash that took place then. Overcoming these small reversals of fortune made him feel invincible. He could do no wrong. He believed that the economic intuition he was endowed with allowed him to make good trading decisions. After a market dip he would verify the fundamentals, and, if they remained sound, he would buy more of the security and lighten up as the market recovered. Looking back at the emerging market bonds between the time Carlos started his involvement with these markets and his last bonus check in December 1997, one sees an upward sloping line, with occasional blips, such as the Mexican devaluation of 1995, followed by an extended rally. One can also see some occasional dips that turned out to be "excellent buying opportunities".

It was the summer of 1998 that undid Carlos – that last dip did not translate into a rally. His track record today includes just one bad quarter – but bad it was. He had earned close to $80 million cumulatively in his previous years. He lost $300 million in just one summer. What happened? When the market started dipping in June, his friendly sources informed him that the sell-off was merely the result of a "liquidation" by a New Jersey hedge fund run by a former Wharton professor. That fund specialized in mortgage securities and had just received instructions to wind down the overall inventory. The inventory included some Russian bonds, mostly because *yield hogs*, as these funds are known, engage in the activity of building a "diversified" portfolio of high-yielding securities.

AVERAGING DOWN

When the market started falling, he accumulated more Russian bonds, at an average of around $52. That was Carlos's trait, average down. The problems, he deemed, had nothing to do with Russia, and it was not some New Jersey fund run by some mad scientist that was going to decide the fate of Russia. "Read my lips: It's a li-qui-da-tion!" he yelled at those who questioned his buying.

By the end of June, his trading revenues for 1998 had dropped from up $60 million to up $20 million. That made him angry. But he calculated that should the market rise back to the pre-New Jersey sell-off, then he would be up $100 million. That was unavoidable, he asserted. These bonds, he said, would never, ever trade below $48. He was risking so little, to possibly make so much.

Then came July. The market dropped a bit more. The benchmark Russian bond was now at $43. His positions were under water, but he increased his stakes. By now he was down $30 million for the year. His bosses were starting to become nervous, but he kept telling them that, after all, Russia would not go under. He repeated the cliché that it was too big to fail. He estimated that bailing them out would cost so little and would benefit the world economy so much that it did not make sense to liquidate his inventory now. "This is the time to buy, not to sell", he said repeatedly. "These bonds are trading very close to their possible default value". In other words, should Russia go into default, and run out of dollars to pay the interest on its debt, these bonds would hardly budge. Where did he get this idea? From discussions with other traders and emerging market economists (or trader-economist hybrids). Carlos put about half his net worth, then $5,000,000, in the Russia Principal Bond. "I will retire on these profits"; he told the stockbroker who executed the trade.

LINES IN THE SAND

The market kept going through the lines in the sand. By early August, they were trading in the 30s. By the middle of August, they were in the 20s. And he was taking no action. He felt that the price on the screen was quite irrelevant in his business of buying "value".

Signs of battle fatigue were starting to show in his behavior. Carlos was getting jumpy and losing some of his composure. He yelled at someone in a meeting: "stop losses are for schmucks! I am not going to buy high and sell low!" During his string of successes he had learned to put down and berate traders of the non-emerging market variety. "Had we gotten out in October 1997 after our heavy loss we would not have had those excellent 1997 results", he was also known to repeat. He also told management: "these bonds trade at very depressed levels. Those who can invest now in these markets would realize wonderful returns". Every morning, Carlos spent an hour discussing the situation with market economists around the globe. They all seemed to present a similar story: this sell-off is overdone.

Carlos's desk experienced losses in other emerging markets as well. He also lost money in the domestic Russian Ruble Bond market. His losses were mounting, but he kept telling his management rumors about very large losses among other banks – larger than his. He felt justified to show that "he fared well relative to the industry". This is a symptom of systemic troubles; it shows that there was an entire community of traders who were conducting the exact same activity. Such statements, that other traders had also gotten into trouble, are self-incriminating. A trader's mental construction should direct him to do precisely *what other people do not do.*

Towards the end of August, the bellwether Russia Principal Bonds were trading below $10. Carlos's net worth was reduced by almost half. He was dismissed. So was his boss, the head of trading. The president of the bank was demoted to a "newly created position". Board members could not understand why the bank had so much exposure to a government that was not paying its own employees – which, disturbingly, included armed soldiers. This was one of the small points that emerging market economists around the globe, from talking to each other so much, forgot to take into account. Veteran trader Marty O'Connell calls this the firehouse effect. He had observed that firemen with much downtime who talk to each other for too long come to agree on many things that an outside, impartial observer, would find ludicrous (they develop political ideas that are very similar). Psychologists give it a fancier name, but my friend Marty has no training in clinical psychology.

The nerdy types at the International Monetary Fund had been taken for a ride by the Russian government who cheated on their account. Let us remember that economists are evaluated on how intelligent they sound, not on a scientific measure of their knowledge of reality. However, the price of the bonds was not fooled. It knew more than the economists, more than the Carloses of the emerging market departments.

Louie, a veteran trader on the neighboring desk who suffered much humiliation by these rich emerging market traders, was there, vindicated. Louie was then a 52-year-old Brooklyn-born-and-raised trader who over three decades survived every single conceivable market cycle. He calmly looked at Carlos being escorted by a security guard to the door like a captured soldier taken to the arena. He muttered in his Brooklyn accent: "*Economics Schmeconomics. It is all market dynamics*".

Carlos is now out of the market. The possibility that history may prove him right (at some point in the future) has nothing to do with the fact that he is a bad trader. He has all of the traits of a thoughtful gentleman, and would be an ideal son-in-law. But he has most of the attributes of the bad trader. And, at any point in time, the richest traders are often the worst traders. This, I will call the *cross-sectional problem*: at a given time in the market, the most profitable traders are likely to be those that are best fit to the latest cycle. This does not happen too often with dentists or pianists – because of the nature of randomness.

John the High-Yield Trader

We met John, Nero's neighbor, in Chapter 1. At the age of 35 he had been on Wall Street as a corporate "high-yield" bonds trader for seven years, since his graduation from Pace Graduate Business School. He rose to head up a team of ten traders in record time – thanks to a jump between two similar Wall Street firms that afforded him a generous profit-sharing contract. The contract allowed him to be paid 20% of his profits, as they stood at the end of each calendar year. In addition, he was allowed to invest his own personal money in his trades – a great privilege.

John is not someone who can be termed as principally intelligent, but he was believed to be endowed with a good measure of business sense. He was said to be "pragmatic" and "professional". He gave the impression that he was born a businessperson, never saying anything remotely unusual or out of place. He remained calm in most circumstances, rarely betraying any form of emotion. Even his occasional cursing (this is Wall Street!) was so much in context that it sounded, well, professional.

John dressed impeccably. This was in part due to his monthly trips to London where his unit had a satellite supervising European high-yield activities. He wore a Saville Row tailored dark business suit, with a Ferragamo tie – enough to convey the impression that he was the epitome of the successful Wall Street professional. Each time Nero ran into him he came away feeling poorly dressed.

John's desk engaged principally in an activity called "high-yield" trading, which consisted in acquiring "cheap" bonds that yielded, say 10%, while the borrowing rate for his institution was 5.5%. It netted a 4.5% revenue, also called *interest rate differential* – which seemed small except that he could leverage himself and multiply such profit by the leverage factor. He did this in various countries, borrowing at the local rate and investing in "risky" assets. It was easy for him to amass over $3 billion dollars in face value of such trade across a variety of continents. He hedged the interest rate exposure by selling U.S., U.K., French, and other government bond futures, thus limiting his bet to the differential between the two instruments. He felt protected by this hedging strategy – cocooned (or so he thought) against those nasty fluctuations in the world's global interest rates.

THE *QUANT* WHO KNEW COMPUTERS AND EQUATIONS

John was assisted by Henry, a foreign *quant* whose English was incomprehensible, but who was believed to be at least equally competent in risk-management methods. John knew no math, he relied on Henry. "His brains and my business sense", he was wont to say. Henry supplied him with risk assessments concerning the overall portfolio. Whenever John felt worried, he would ask Henry for another freshly updated report. Henry was a graduate student in Operations Research when John hired him. His specialty was a field called Computational Finance, which, as its name indicates, seems to focus solely on running computer programs overnight. Henry's income went from $50,000 to $600,000 in three years.

Most of the profit John generated for the institution was not attributable to the interest rate differential between the instruments described above. It came from the changes in the value of the securities John held, mostly because many other traders were acquiring them to imitate John's trading strategy (thus causing the price of these assets to rise). The interest rate differential was getting closer to what John believed was "fair value". John believed that the methods he used to calculate "fair value" were sound. He was backed by an entire department that helped him analyze and determine which bonds were attractive and offered capital appreciation potential. It was normal for him to be earning these large profits over time.

John made steady money for his employers, perhaps even better than steady. Every year the revenues he generated almost doubled as compared to the previous year. During his last year, his income experienced a quantum leap as he saw the capital allocated to his trades swell beyond his wildest expectations. His bonus check was for $10 million (pretax, which would generate close to a $5 million total tax bill). John's personal net worth reached $1 million at the age of 32. By the age of 35 it had exceeded $16 million. Most of it came from the accumulation of bonuses – but a sizeable share came from profits on his personal portfolio. Of the $16 million, about $14 million he insisted in keeping invested in his business. They allowed him, thanks to the leverage (i.e., use of borrowed money), to keep a portfolio of $50 million involved in his trades, with $36 million borrowed from the bank. The effect of the leverage is that a small loss would be compounded and would wipe him out.

It took only a few days for the $14 million to turn into thin air – and for John to lose his job at the same time. It all happened during the summer of 1998, with the meltdown of high-yield bond values. Markets went into a volatile phase in which nearly everything he had invested in went against him *at the same time*. His hedges no longer worked out. He was mad at Henry for not having figured out that these events could happen. Perhaps there was a bug in the program.

His reaction to the first losses was, characteristically, to ignore the market. "One would go crazy if one were to listen to the mood swings of the market", he said. What he meant by that statement was that the "noise" was mean reverting, and would likely be offset by "noise" in the opposite direction. That was the translation in plain English of what Henry explained to him. But the "noise" kept adding up in the same direction.

As in a biblical cycle, it took seven years to make John a hero and just seven days to make him an idiot. John is now a pariah; he is out of a job and his telephone calls are not returned. Many of his friends were in the same situation. How? With all that information available to him, his perfect track record (and therefore, in his eyes, an above average intelligence and skill-set) and the benefit of sophisticated mathematics, how could he have failed? Is it perhaps possible that he forgot about the shadowy figure of randomness?

It took a long time for John to figure out what had happened, owing to the rapidity with which the events unfolded and his state of shellshock. The dip in the market was not very large. It was just that his leverage was enormous. What was more shocking for him was that all their calculations gave the event a probability of 1 in 1,000,000,000,000,000,000,000,000 years. Henry called that a "ten sigma" event. The fact that Henry doubled the odds did not seem to matter. It made the probability 2 in 1,000,000,000,000,000,000,000,000 years.

When will John recover from the ordeal? Probably never. The reason is not because John lost money. Losing money is something good traders are accustomed to. It is because he blew up; he lost more than he planned to lose. His personal confidence was wiped out. But there is another reason why John may never recover. The reason is that John was never a trader in the first place. He is one of those people who happened to be there when it all happened.

Following the incident, John regarded himself "ruined"; yet his net worth is still close to $1 million, which could be the envy of more than 99.9% of the inhabitants of our planet. Yet there is a difference between a wealth level reached from *above* and a wealth reached from *below*. The road from $16 million to $1 million is not as pleasant as the one from 0 to $1 million. In addition, John is full of shame; he still worries about running into old friends on the street.

His employer should perhaps be most unhappy with the overall outcome. John pulled some money out of the episode, the $1 million he had saved. He should be thankful that the episode did not cost him anything – except the emotional drain. His net worth did not become negative. That was not the case for his last employer. John had earned for the employers, New York investment banks, around $250 million in the course of the seven years. He lost more than $600 million for his last employer in barely a few days.

THE TRAITS THEY SHARED

The reader needs to be warned that not all of the emerging market and high-yield traders talk and behave like Carlos and John. Only the most successful ones – alas, or perhaps those who were the most successful during the 1992–1998 bull cycle.

At their age, both John and Carlos still have the chance to make a career. It would be wise for them to look outside of the financial markets. The odds are that they will not survive the incident. Why? Because by discussing the situation with each of them, one can rapidly see that they share the traits of the *acute successful randomness fool*. What is more worrisome is that their bosses and employers shared the same trait. They, too, are permanently out of the market. We will see throughout this book what characterizes the trait. Again, there may not be a clear definition for it, but you can recognize it when you see it. No matter what John and Carlos do, they will remain fools of randomness.

A Review of Market Fools of Randomness Constants

Most of the traits partake of the same Table P.1 right-column–left-column confusion; how they are fooled by randomness. Below is a brief outline of them:

*An overestimation of the accuracy of their beliefs in some measure,
either economic (Carlos) or statistical (John).* They never considered that the fact that trading on economic variables has worked
in the past may have been merely coincidental, or, perhaps even
worse, that economic analysis was fit to past events to mask the
random element in it. Carlos entered the market at a time when it
worked, but he never tested for periods when markets did the
opposite of sound economic analysis. There were periods when
economics failed traders, and others when it helped them.

The U.S. dollar was overpriced (i.e. the foreign currencies were
undervalued) in the early 1980s. Traders who used their economic
intuitions and bought foreign currencies were wiped out. But later
those who did so got rich (members of the first crop were bust). It is
random! Likewise, those who "shorted" Japanese stocks in the late
1980s suffered the same fate – few survived to recoup their losses
during the collapse of the 1990s. At the time of writing, there is a
group of operators called "macro" traders who are dropping like
flies, with "legendary" (rather, lucky) investor Julian Robertson
closing shop in 2000 after having been a star until then. Our
discussion of survivorship bias will enlighten us further, but, clearly,
there is nothing less rigorous than their seemingly rigorous use of
economic analysis to trade.

A tendency to get married to positions.   There is a saying that bad
traders divorce their spouse sooner than abandon their positions.
Loyalty to ideas is not a good thing for traders, scientists – or
anyone.

The tendency to change their story.   They become investors "for the
long haul" when they are losing money, switching back and forth
between traders and investors to fit recent reversals of fortune. The
difference between a trader and an investor lies in the duration of the
bet, and the corresponding size. There is absolutely nothing wrong
with investing "for the long haul", provided one does not mix it with
short-term trading – it is just that many people become long-term
investors after they lost money, postponing their decision to sell, as
part of their denial.

No precise game plan ahead of time as to what to do in the event of losses. They simply were not aware of such a possibility. Both bought more bonds after the market declined sharply, but not in response to a predetermined plan.

Absence of critical thinking expressed in absence of revision of their stance with "stop losses". Middlebrow traders do not like selling when it is "even better value". They did not consider that perhaps their method of determining value is wrong, rather than the market failing to accommodate their measure of value. They may be right, but, perhaps, some allowance for the possibility of their methods being flawed was not made. For all his flaws, we will see that Soros seems rarely to examine an unfavorable outcome without testing his own framework of analysis.

Denial. When the losses occurred there was no clear acceptance of what had happened. The price on the screen lost its reality in favor of some abstract "value". In classic denial mode, the usual "this is only the result of liquidation, distress sales" was proffered. They continuously ignored the message from reality.

How could traders who made every single mistake in the book become so successful? Because of a simple principle concerning randomness. This is one manifestation of the survivorship bias. We tend to think that traders make money *because* they are good. Perhaps we have turned the causality on its head; we consider them good just because they make money. One can make money in the financial markets totally out of randomness.

Both Carlos and John belong to the class of people who benefited from a market cycle. It was not merely because they were involved in the right markets. It was because they had a bent in their style that closely fitted the properties of the rallies experienced in their market during the episode. They were *dip buyers*. That happened, in hindsight, to be the trait that was the most desirable between 1992 and the summer of 1998 in the specific markets in which the two men specialized. Most of those who happened to have that specific trait, over the course of that segment of history, dominated the market. Their score was higher and they replaced people who, perhaps, were better traders.

Naïve Evolutionary Theories

This story illustrates how bad traders have a short- and medium-term survival advantage over good traders. Next we take the argument to a higher level of generality. One must be either blind or foolish to reject the theories of Darwinian self-selection. However, the simplicity of the concept has drawn segments of amateurs (as well as a few professional scientists) into blindly believing in continuous and infallible Darwinism in all fields, which includes economics.

The biologist Jacques Monod bemoaned a couple of decades ago that everyone believes himself an expert on evolution (the same can be said about the financial markets); things have gotten worse. Many amateurs believe that plants and animals reproduce on a one-way route towards perfection. Translating the idea in social terms, they believe that companies and organizations are, thanks to competition (and the discipline of the quarterly report), irreversibly heading towards betterment. The strongest will survive; the weakest will become extinct. As to investors and traders, they believe that by letting them compete, the best will prosper and the worst will go learn a new craft (like pumping gas or, sometimes, dentistry).

Things are not as simple as that. We will ignore the basic misuse of Darwinian ideas in the fact that organizations do not reproduce like living members of nature – Darwinian ideas are about reproductive fitness, not about survival. The problem comes, as everything else in this book, from randomness. Zoologists found that once randomness is injected into a system, the results can be quite surprising: what seems to be an evolution may be merely a diversion, and possibly regression. For instance, Steven Jay Gould (admittedly more of a popularizer than a genuine scientist) found ample evidence of what he calls "genetic noise", or "negative mutations", thus causing the wrath of some of his colleagues (he took the idea a little too far). An academic debate ensued, plotting Gould against colleagues like Dawkins who were considered by their peers as better trained in the mathematics of randomness. Negative mutations are traits that survive in spite of being worse, from the reproductive fitness standpoint, than the ones they replaced. However, they cannot be expected to last more than a few generations (under what is called temporal aggregation).

Furthermore, things can get even more surprising when randomness changes in shape, as with regime switches. A regime switch corresponds to situations when all of the attributes of a system change to the point of it becoming unrecognizable to the observer. Darwinian fitness applies to species developing over a very long time, not observed over a short term – time aggregation eliminates much of the effects of randomness; things (I read *noise*) balance out over the long run, as people say.

Owing to the abrupt rare events, we do not live in a world where things "converge" continuously towards betterment. Nor do things in life move *continuously* at all. The belief in continuity was ingrained in our scientific culture until the early twentieth century. It was said that *nature does not make jumps*; people quote this in well-sounding Latin: *natura no facit saltus*. It is generally attributed to the eighteenth-century botanist Linnaeus who obviously got it all wrong. It was also used by Leibniz as a justification of calculus, as he believed that things are continuous no matter the resolution at which we look at them. Like many well-sounding "make sense" types of statements (such dynamics made perfect intellectual sense), it turned out to be entirely wrong, as it was denied by quantum mechanics. We discovered that, in the very small, particles jump (discretely) between states; they do not slide between them.

CAN EVOLUTION BE FOOLED BY RANDOMNESS?

We end this chapter with the following thought. Recall that someone with only casual knowledge about the problems of randomness would believe that an animal is at the maximum fitness for the conditions of his time. This is not what evolution means; *on average* animals will be fit, but not every single one of them, and not at all times. Just as an animal could have survived because its sample path was lucky, the "best" operators in a given business can come from a subset of operators who survived because of over-fitness to a sample path – a sample path that was free of the evolutionary rare event. One vicious attribute is that the longer these animals can go without encountering the rare event, the more vulnerable they will be to it. We said that should one extend time to infinity, then, by *ergodicity*, that event will happen with certainty –

the species will be wiped out! For evolution means fitness to one and only time series, not the average of all the possible environments.

By some viciousness of the structure of randomness, a profitable person like John, someone who is a pure loser in the long run and correspondingly unfit for survival, presents a high degree of eligibility in the short run and has the propensity to multiply his genes. Recall the hormonal effect on posture and its signaling effect to other potential mates. His success (or pseudo-success owing to its fragility) will show in his features as a beacon. An innocent potential mate will be fooled into thinking (unconditionally) that he has a superior genetic makeup, until the following rare event. Solon seems to have gotten the point; but try to explain the problem to a naïve business Darwinist – or your rich neighbor across the street.

SIX

SKEWNESS AND ASYMMETRY

We introduce the concept of skewness: why the terms "bull" and
"bear" have limited meaning outside of zoology. A vicious child
wrecks the structure of randomness. An introduction to the
problem of epistemological opacity. The penultimate step
before the problem of induction.

The Median Is Not the Message

The writer and scientist Steven Jay Gould (who, for a while, was my role model), was once diagnosed with a deadly form of cancer of the lining of the stomach. The first piece of information he received about his odds of making it was that the *median* survival for the ailment is approximately eight months; information he felt akin to Isaiah's injunction to King Hezekiah to put his house in order in preparation for death.

Now a medical diagnosis, particularly one of such severity, can motivate people to do intensive research, particularly those prolific writers like Gould who needed more time with us to complete a few book projects. The further research by Gould uncovered a very different story to the information he had initially been given; mainly that the *expected* (i.e., average) survival was considerably higher than eight months. It came to his notice that *expected* and *median* do not mean the same thing at all. Median means roughly that 50% of the people die before eight months and 50% survive longer than eight months. But those who survive would live considerably longer, generally going about life just like a regular person and fulfilling the average 73.4 or so years predicted by insurance mortality tables.

There is asymmetry. Those who die do so very early in the game, while those who live go on living very long. Whenever there is asymmetry in outcomes, the *average* survival has nothing to do with the *median* survival. This prompted Gould, who thus discovered the concept of skewness, to write his heartfelt piece "The Median is Not the Message". His point is that the concept of median used in medical research does not characterize a probability distribution.

I will simplify Gould's point by introducing the concept of *mean* (also called *expectation*) as follows by using a less morbid example, that of gambling. I will give an example of both asymmetric odds and asymmetric outcomes to explain the point. Asymmetric odds means that probabilities are not 50% for each event, but that the probability on one side is higher than the probability on the other. Asymmetric outcomes mean that the payoffs are not equal.

Assume I engage in a gambling strategy that has 999 chances in 1,000 of making $1 (event A) and 1 chance in 1,000 of losing $10,000 (event B), as in Table 6.1.

Table 6.1

Event	Probability	Outcome	Expectation
A	999/1000	$1	$.999
B	1/1000	−$10,000	−$10.00
		Total	−$9.001

My expectation is a loss of close to $9 (obtained by multiplying the probabilities by the corresponding outcomes). The *frequency* or *probability* of the loss, in and by itself, is totally irrelevant; it needs to be judged in connection with the *magnitude* of the outcome. Here A is far more likely than B. Odds are that we would make money by betting for event A, but it is not a good idea to do so.

This point is rather common and simple; it is understood by anyone making a simple bet. Yet I had to struggle all my life with people in the financial markets who do not seem to internalize it. I am not talking of novices; I am talking of people with advanced degrees (albeit MBAs) who cannot come to grips with the difference.

How could people miss such a point? Why do they confuse probability and expectation, that is, probability and probability times the payoff? Mainly because much of people's schooling comes from examples in symmetric environments, like a coin-toss, where such a difference does not matter. In fact the so-called "Bell Curve" that seems to have found universal use in society is entirely symmetric. More on that later.

Bull and Bear Zoology

The general press floods us with concepts like *bullish* and *bearish* as these mean to refer to the effect of higher (bullish) or lower (bearish) prices in the financial markets. But also we hear people saying "I am *bullish* on Johnny" or "I am *bearish* on that guy Nassim in the back who seems incomprehensible to me", to denote the belief in the likelihood of someone's rise in life. I have to say that the notion *bullish* or *bearish* are often hollow words with no application in a world of randomness – particularly if such a world, like ours, presents asymmetric outcomes.

When I was in the employment of the New York office of a large investment house, I was subjected on occasions to the harrying weekly "discussion meeting", which gathered most professionals of the New York trading room. I do not conceal that I was not fond of such gatherings, and not only because they cut into my gym time. While the meetings included traders, that is, people who are judged on their numerical performance, it was mostly a forum for salespeople (people capable of charming customers), and the category of entertainers called Wall Street "economists" or "strategists" who make pronouncements on the fate of the markets, but do not engage in any form of risk taking, thus having their success dependent on rhetoric rather than actually testable facts. During the discussion, people were supposed to present their opinions on the state of the world. To me, the meeting was pure intellectual pollution. Everyone had a story, a theory, and insights that they wanted others to share. I resent the person who, without having done much homework in libraries, thinks that he is onto something rather original and insightful on a given subject matter (and respect people with scientific minds like my friend Stan Jonas who feel compelled to spend their nights reading wholesale on a subject matter, trying to figure out what was done on the subject by others before emitting an opinion – would the reader listen to the opinion of a doctor who does not read medical papers?).

I have to confess that my optimal strategy (to soothe my boredom and allergy to confident platitudes) was to speak as much as I could, while totally avoiding listening to other people's replies by trying to solve equations in my head. Speaking too much would help me clarify my mind, and, with a little bit of luck, I would not be "invited" back (that is, forced to attend) the following week.

I was once asked in one of those meetings to express my views on the stock market. I stated, not without a modicum of pomp, that I believed that the market would go slightly up over the next week with a high probability. How high? "About 70%". Clearly, that was a very strong opinion. But then someone interjected "But, Nassim, you just boasted being short a very large quantity of SP500 futures, making a bet that the market would go down. What made you change your mind?". "I did not change my mind! I have a lot of faith in my bet! (audience laughing). As a matter of fact I now feel like selling even more!" The other employees in the room seemed utterly confused. "Are you bullish or are you bearish?" I was asked by the strategist. I replied that I could not understand the words "bullish" and "bearish" outside of their purely zoological consideration. Just as with events A and B in the preceding example, my opinion was that the market was more likely to go up ("I would be bullish"), but that it was preferable to short it ("I would be bearish"), because, in the event of its going down, it could go down a lot. Suddenly, the few traders in the room understood my opinion and started voicing similar opinions. And I was not forced to come back to the following discussion.

Let us assume that the reader shared my opinion, that the market over the next week had a 70% probability of going up and 30% probability of going down. However, let us say that it would go up by 1% on average, while it could go down by an average of 10%. What would the reader do? Is the reader *bullish* or is he *bearish*?

Table 6.2

Event	Probability	Outcome	Expectation
Market goes up	70%	Up 1%	0.7
Market goes down	30%	Down 10%	−3.00
		Total	−2.3

Accordingly, *bullish* or *bearish* are terms used by people who do not engage in practicing uncertainty, like the television commentators, or those who have no experience in handling risk. Alas, investors and businesses are not paid in probabilities, they are paid in dollars. Accordingly, it is not how likely an event is to happen that matters, it is how much is made when it happens that should be the consideration. How frequent the profit is irrelevant; it is the magnitude of the outcome that counts. It is a pure accounting fact that, aside from the commentators, very few people take home a check linked to how *often* they are right or wrong. What they get is a profit or loss. As to the commentators, their success is linked to how often they are right or wrong. This category includes the "chief strategists" of major investment banks the public can see on T.V., who are nothing better than entertainers. They are famous, seem reasoned in their speech, plow you with numbers, but, functionally, they are there to entertain – for their predictions to have any validity they would need a statistical testing framework. Their fame is not the result of some elaborate test but rather the result of their presentation skills.

AN ARROGANT 29-YEAR-OLD SON

Outside of the need for entertainment in these shallow meetings I have resisted voicing a "market call" as a trader, which caused some personal strain with some of my friends and relatives. One day a friend of my father – of the rich and confident variety – called me during his New York visit (to set the elements of pecking order straight, he hinted right away during the call that he came by Concorde, with some derogatory comment on the comfort of such method of transportation). He wanted to pick my brain on the state of a collection of financial markets. I truly had no opinion, nor had made the effort to formulate any, nor was I remotely interested in markets. The gentleman kept plowing me with questions on the state of economies, on the European central banks; these were precise questions no doubt aiming to compare my opinion to that of some other "expert" handling his account at one of the large New York investment firms. I neither concealed that I had no clue, nor did I seem sorry about it. I was not interested in markets ("yes, I am a trader") and did not make predictions, period. I went on to explain to him some of my ideas on the structure of randomness and the verificability of market calls but he wanted a more precise statement of what the European bond markets would do by the Christmas season.

He came under the impression that I was pulling his leg; it almost damaged the relationship between my father and his rich and confident friend. For the gentleman called him with the following grievance: "When I ask a lawyer a legal question, he answers me with courtesy and precision. When I ask a doctor a medical question, he gives me his opinion. No specialist ever gives me disrespect. Your insolent and conceited 29-year-old son is playing *prima donna* and refuses to answer me about the direction of the market!"

RARE EVENTS

The best description of my lifelong business in the market is "skewed bets", that is, I try to benefit from rare events, events that do not tend to repeat themselves frequently, but, accordingly, present a large payoff when they occur. I try to make money infrequently, as infrequently as possible, simply because I believe that rare events are not fairly valued, and that the rarer the event, the more undervalued it will be in price.

Why? Because of a psychological bias; people who surrounded me in my career were too focused on memorizing section 2 of the *Wall Street*

Journal during their train ride to reflect properly on the attributes of random events. Or perhaps they watched too many gurus on television. Or perhaps they spent too much time upgrading their PalmPilot. Even some experienced trading veterans do not seem to get the point that frequencies do not matter. Jim Rogers, a "legendary" investor, made the following statement:

> *I don't buy options. Buying options is another way to go to the poor-house. Someone did a study for the SEC and discovered that 90 percent of all options expire as losses. Well, I figured out that if 90 percent of all long option positions lost money, that meant that 90 percent of all short option positions make money. If I want to use options to be bearish, I sell calls.*

Visibly, the statistic that 90% of all option positions lost money is meaningless, (i.e., the *frequency*) if we do not take into account *how much* money is made on average during the remaining 10%. If we make 50 times our bet on average when the option is in the money, then I can safely make the statement that buying options is another way to go to the palazzo rather than the poorhouse. Mr Jim Rogers seems to have gone very far in life for someone who does not distinguish between probability and expectation (strangely, he was the partner of George Soros, a complex man who thrived on rare events – more on him later).

One such rare event is the stock market crash of 1987, which made me as a trader and allowed me the luxury of becoming involved in all manner of scholarship. Nero of the smaller house in Chapter 1 aims to get out of harm's way by avoiding exposure to rare events – a mostly defensive approach. I am far more aggressive than Nero and go one step further; I have organized my career and business in such a way as to be able to benefit from them. In other words, I aim at profiting from the rare event, with my asymmetric bets.

SYMMETRY AND SCIENCE

In most disciplines, such asymmetry does not matter. Unfortunately, the techniques used in finance are often imported from other areas – finance is still a young discipline (it is certainly not yet a "science"). People in most fields outside of finance do not have problems eliminating extreme values from their sample, when the difference in payoff between different outcomes is not significant, which is generally the case in education and medicine. A professor who computes the average of his students' grades removes the highest and lowest observations, which he would call *outliers*, and takes the average of the remaining ones, without this being an unsound practice. A casual weather forecaster does the same with extreme temperatures – an unusual occurrence might be deemed to skew the overall result (though we will see that this may turn out to be a mistake when it comes to forecasting future properties of the ice cap). So people in finance borrow the technique and ignore infrequent events, not noticing that the effect of a rare event can bankrupt a company.

Many scientists in the physical world are also subject to such foolishness, misreading statistics. One flagrant example is in the global-warming debate. Many scientists failed to notice it in its early stages as they removed from their sample the spikes in temperature, under the belief that these were not likely to recur. It may be a good idea to take out the extremes when computing the average temperatures for vacation scheduling. But it does not work when we study the physical properties of the weather. These scientists initially ignored the fact that these spikes, although rare, had the effect of adding disproportionately to the cumulative melting of the ice cap. Just as in finance, an event, although rare, that brings large consequences cannot just be ignored.

Figure 6.1 shows a series of points starting with an initial level W_0 and ending at the period concerned W_t. It can also be seen as the performance, hypothetical or realized, of your favorite trading strategy, the track record of an investment manager, the price of a foot of average Palazzo real estate in Renaissance Florence, the price series of the Mongolian stock market, or the difference between the U.S. and Mongolian stock markets. It is composed of a given number of sequential observations W_1, W_2, etc., ordered in such a way that the one to the right comes *after* the one to the left.

If we were dealing with a deterministic world – that is, a world stripped of randomness (the right-column world in Table P.1 on page 3), and we knew with certainty that it was the case, things would be rather

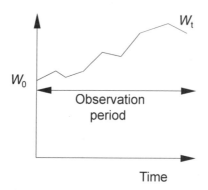

Figure 6.1   A Primer on Time Series.

᠁sy. The pattern of the series would reveal considerable and predictive information. You could tell with precision what would happen one day ahead, one year ahead, and perhaps even a decade ahead. We would not even need a statistician; a second-rate engineer would do. He does not even need to be armed with a modern degree; someone with nineteenth-century training under Laplace would be able to solve the equations, called *differential equations*, or, equivalently, *equations of motion* – since we are studying the dynamics of an entity whose position depends on time.

If we were dealing with a world where randomness is charted, things would be easy as well, given that there is an entire field created for that called *Econometrics* or *Time Series Analysis*. You would call a friendly econometrician (my experience of econometricians is that they are usually polite and friendly to practitioners). He would run the data in his software, and provide you with diagnostics that would tell you if it is worth investing in the trader generating such a track record, or if it is worth pursuing the given trading strategy. You can even buy the student version of his software for under $999 and run it yourself during the next rainy weekend.

But we are not sure that the world we live in is well charted. We will see that the judgment derived from the analysis of these past attributes may on occasion be relevant. But it may be meaningless; it could on occasion mislead you and take you in the opposite direction. Sometimes market data becomes a simple trap; it shows you the opposite of its nature, simply to get you to invest in the security or mismanage your risks. Currencies that exhibit the largest historical stability, for example, are the most prone to crashes. This was bitterly discovered in the summer of 1997 by investors who chose the safety of the pegged currencies of Malaysia, Indonesia, and Thailand (they were pegged to the U.S. dollar in a manner to exhibit no volatility, until their sharp, sudden, and brutal devaluations).

We could be either too lax or too stringent in accepting past information as a prediction of the future. As a skeptic, I reject a sole time series of the past as an indication of future performance; I need a lot more than data. My major reason is the *rare event*, but I have plenty of others.

On the surface, my statement here may seem to contradict earlier discussions, where I blame people for not learning enough from history. The problem is that we read too much into shallow recent history, with statements like "this has never happened before", but not from history in general (things that never happened before in one area tend eventually to happen). In other words history teaches us that things that never happened before do happen. It can teach us a lot outside of the narrowly defined time series; the broader the look, the better the lesson. In other words, history teaches us to avoid the brand of naïve empiricism that consists of learning from casual historical facts.

The Rare Event Fallacy

THE MOTHER OF ALL DECEPTIONS

The rare event, owing to its dissimulative nature, can take a variety of shapes. It is in Mexico that it was spotted first, where it was called by academics the *peso problem*. Econometricians were puzzled by the behavior of the Mexican economic variables during the 1980s. The money supply, interest rates, or some similar measure of small relevance to the story exhibited some moody behavior, thwarting many of their efforts at modeling them. These indicators erratically switched between periods of stability to brief bursts of turbulence without warning.

By generalization, I started to label a rare event as any behavior where the adage "beware of calm waters" can hold. Popular wisdom often warns of the old neighbor who appears to remain courtly and reserved, the model of an excellent citizen, until you see his picture in the national paper as a deranged killer who went on a rampage. Until then, he was not known to have committed any transgression. There was no way to predict that such pathological behavior could emanate from such a nice person. I associate rare events with any misunderstanding of the risks derived from a narrow interpretation of past time series.

Rare events are always unexpected, otherwise they would not occur. The typical case is as follows. You invest in a hedge fund that enjoys stable returns and no volatility, until one day, you receive a letter starting with "An unforeseen and *unexpected* event, deemed a rare occurrence ..." (emphasis mine). But rare events exist precisely because they are unexpected. They are generally caused by panics, themselves the results of liquidations (the investors rushing to the door simultaneously by dumping anything they can put their hands on as fast as possible). If the fund manager or trader expected it, he and his like-minded peers would not have invested in it, and the rare event would not have taken place.

The rare event is not limited to one security. It can readily affect the performance of a portfolio. For example, many traders engage in the purchase of mortgage securities and hedge them in some manner to offset the risks and eliminate the volatility, hoping to derive some profits in excess of the Treasury bond returns (which is used as the benchmark of the minimum expected returns on an investment). They use computer programs and draw meaningful assistance from Ph.D.s in applied mathematics, astrophysics, particle physics, electrical engineering, fluid dynamics, or sometimes (though rarely) plain Ph.D.s in Finance. Such a portfolio shows stable returns for long periods. Then, suddenly, as if by accident (I consider that *no* accident), the portfolio drops by 40% of its value when you expect, at the worst, a 4% drop. You call the manager to express your anger and he tells you that it was not his fault, but somehow the relationship dramatically changed (literally). He will also point out to you that similar funds also experienced the same problems.

Recall that some economists call the rare event a "peso problem". The designation peso problem does not appear to be undeservedly stereotypical. Things have not gotten better since the early 1980s with the currency of the U.S.'s southern neighbor. Long periods of stability draw hordes of bank currency traders and hedge fund operators to the calm waters of the Mexican peso; they enjoy owning the currency because of the high interest rate it commands. Then they "unexpectedly" blow up, lose money for investors, lose their jobs and switch careers. Then a new period of stability sets in. New currency traders come in with no memory of the bad event. They are drawn to the Mexican peso, and the story repeats itself.

It is an oddity that most fixed income financial instruments present rare events. In the spring of 1998, I spent two hours explaining to a then-important hedge fund operator the notion of the *peso problem*. I went to great lengths to explain to him that the concept was generalized to every form of investment that was based on a naïve interpretation of the volatility of past time series. The reply was: "You are perfectly right. We do not touch the Mexican peso. We only invest in the Russian ruble". He blew up a few months later. Until then, the Russian ruble carried attractive interest rates, which invited yield hogs of all types to get involved. He and other holders of investments denominated in rubles lost close to 97% of their investment during the summer of 1998.

We saw in Chapter 3 that the dentist does not like volatility as it causes a high incidence of negative pangs. The closer he observes his performance, the more pain he will experience owing to the greater variability at a higher resolution. Accordingly investors, merely for emotional reasons, will be drawn into strategies that experience *rare but large* variations. It is called pushing randomness under the rug.

We can look at other aspects of the problem; think of someone involved in scientific research. Day after day, he will engage in dissecting mice in his laboratory, away from the rest of the world. He could try and try for years and years without anything to show for it. His significant other might lose patience with the *loser* who comes home every night smelling of mice urine. Until bingo, one day he comes up with a result. Someone observing the time series of his occupation would see absolutely no gain, while every day would bring him closer *in probability* to the end result.

The same with publishers; they can publish dog after dog without their business model being the least questionable, if once every decade they hit on a Harry Potter string of super-best-sellers – provided of course that they publish quality work that has a small probability of being of very high appeal.

In the markets, there is a category of traders who have *inverse* rare events, for whom volatility is often a bearer of good news. These traders lose money frequently, but in small amounts, and make money rarely, but in large amounts. I call them crisis hunters. I am happy to be one of them.

WHY DON'T STATISTICIANS DETECT RARE EVENTS?

Statistics to the layman can appear rather complex, but the concept behind what is used today is so simple that my French mathematician friends call it deprecatorily "cuisine". It is all based on one simple notion; the more information you have, the more you are confident about the outcome. Now the problem; by how much? Common statistical method is based on the steady augmentation of the confidence level, in nonlinear proportion to the number of observations. That is, for an n times increase in the sample size, we increase our knowledge by the square root of n. Suppose I am drawing from an urn containing red and black balls. My confidence level about the relative proportion of red and black balls, after 20 drawings is not twice the one I have after 10 drawings; it is merely multiplied by the square root of 2 (that is, 1.41).

Where statistics becomes complicated, and fails us, is when we have distributions that are not symmetric, like the urn above. If there is a very small probability of finding a red ball in an urn dominated by black ones, then our knowledge about the *absence* of red balls will increase very slowly – more slowly than at the expected square root of n rate. On the other hand our knowledge of the *presence* of red balls will dramatically improve once one of them is found. This asymmetry in knowledge is not trivial; it is central in this book – it is a central philosophical problem for such people as Hume and Karl Popper (on that, later).

To assess an investor's performance, we either need more astute, and less intuitive, techniques, or we may have to limit our assessments to situations where our judgment is independent of the frequency of these events.

A MISCHIEVOUS CHILD REPLACES THE BLACK BALLS

But there is even worse news. In some cases, if the incidence of red balls is itself randomly distributed, we will never get to know the composition of the urn. This is called *the problem of stationarity*. Think of an urn that is hollow at the bottom. As I am sampling from it, and without my being aware of it, some mischievous child is adding balls of one color or another. My inference thus becomes insignificant. I may infer that the red balls represent 50% of the urn while the mischievous child, hearing me, would swiftly replace all the red balls with black ones. This makes much of our knowledge derived through statistics quite shaky.

The very same effect takes place in the market. We take past history as a single homogeneous sample and believe that we have considerably increased our knowledge of the future from the observation of the sample of the past. What if vicious children were changing the composition of the urn? In other words, what if things have changed?

I have studied and practiced econometrics for more than half my life (since I was 19), both in the classroom and in the activity of a quantitative derivatives trader. The "science" of econometrics consists of the application of statistics to samples taken at different periods of time, which we called *time series*. It is based on studying the time series of economic variables, data, and other matters. In the beginning, when I knew close to nothing (that is even less than today), I wondered whether the time series reflecting the activity of people now dead or retired should matter for predicting the future. Econometricians who knew a lot more than I did about these matters asked no such question; this hinted that it was in all likelihood a stupid inquiry. One prominent econometrician, Hashem Pesaran, answered a similar question by recommending to do "more and better econometrics". I am now convinced that, perhaps, most of econometrics could be useless – much of what financial statisticians know would not be worth knowing. For a sum of zeros, even repeated a billion times, remains zero; likewise an accumulation of research and gains in complexity will lead to naught if there is no firm ground beneath it. Studying the European markets of the 1990s will certainly be of great help to a historian; but what kind of inference can we make now that the structure of the institutions and the markets has changed so much?

Note that the economist Robert Lucas dealt a blow to econometrics by arguing that if people were rational then their rationality would cause them to figure out predictable patterns from the past and adapt, so that past information would be completely useless for predicting the future (the argument, phrased in a very mathematical form, earned him a Nobel Memorial Prize in Economics). We are human and act according to our knowledge, which integrates past data. I can translate his point with the following analogy. If rational traders detect a pattern of stocks rising on Mondays, then, immediately such a pattern becomes detectable, it would be ironed out by people buying on Friday in anticipation of such an effect. There is no point searching for patterns that are available to everyone with a brokerage account; once detected, they would be ironed out.

Somehow, what came to be known as the *Lucas critique* was not carried through by the "scientists". It was confidently believed that the scientific successes of the industrial revolution could be carried through into the social sciences, particularly with such movements as Marxism. Pseudoscience came with a collection of idealistic nerds who tried to create a tailor-made society, the epitome of which is the central planner. Economics was the most likely candidate for such use of science; you can disguise charlatanism under the weight of equations, and nobody can catch you since there is no such thing as a controlled experiment. Now the spirit of such methods, called *scientism* by its detractors (like myself), continued past Marxism, into the discipline of finance as a few technicians thought that their mathematical knowledge could lead them to understand markets. The practice of "financial engineering" came along with massive doses of pseudoscience. Practitioners of these methods measure risks, using the tool of past history as an indication of the future. We will just say at this point that the mere possibility of the distributions not being stationary makes the entire concept seem like a costly (perhaps *very costly*) mistake. This leads us to a more fundamental question: the problem of induction, to which we will turn in the next chapter.

SEVEN

THE PROBLEM OF INDUCTION

On the chromodynamics of swans. Taking Solon's warning into some philosophical territory. How Victor Niederhoffer taught me empiricism; I added deduction. Why it is not scientific to take science seriously. Soros promotes Popper. That bookstore on 21st and Fifth Avenue. Pascal's wager.

From Bacon to Hume

Now we discuss this problem viewed from the broader standpoint of the philosophy of scientific knowledge. There is a problem in inference well known as the problem of induction. It is a problem that has been haunting science for a long time, but science has not been as harmed by it as the financial markets. Why? Because the randomness content compounds its effects. Nowhere is the problem of induction more relevant than in my world of finance – and nowhere has it been as ignored!

CYGNUS ATRATUS

In his *Treatise on Human Nature*, the Scots philosopher David Hume posed the issue in the following way (as rephrased in the now famous *black swan problem* by John Stuart Mill): *No amount of observations of white swans can allow the inference that all swans are white, but the observation of a single black swan is sufficient to refute that conclusion.*

Hume had been irked by the fact that science in his day (the eighteenth century) had experienced a swing from scholasticism, entirely based on deductive reasoning (no emphasis on the observation of the real world) to, owing to Francis Bacon, an overreaction into naïve and unstructured empiricism. Bacon had argued against "spinning the cobweb of learning" with little practical result. Science had shifted, thanks to Bacon, into an emphasis on empirical observation. The problem is that, without a proper method, empirical observations can lead you astray. Hume came to warn us against such knowledge, and to stress the need for some rigor in the gathering and interpretation of knowledge – what is called epistemology (from *episteme*, Greek for learning). Hume is the first modern *epistemologist*, (epistemologists are often called methodologists or philosophers of science). What I am writing here is not strictly true, for Hume said things far worse than that; he was an obsessive skeptic and never believed that a link between two items could be truly established as being causal. But we will tone him down a bit for this book.

NIEDERHOFFER, VICTORIAN GENTLEMAN

It is worth noting that finance has its Francis Bacon in the person of Victor Niederhoffer. He was the very first to stand against the *cobweb of learning* of the University of Chicago and the efficient market religion of the 1960s, when it was at its worst. In contrast with the scholasticism of financial theorists, he looked at data in search of anomalies – and found enough of them to be able to conduct a successful career in randomness and deliver an insightful book, *The Education of a Speculator*. Since then, an entire industry of such operators, called "statistical arbitrageurs", flourished, the major and most successful ones were initially his trainees. While Niederhoffer had a publicized hiccup, some of his trainees fared well because they added rigor and *methodology* to their statistical inference. In other words, Niederhoffer's empiricism missed just a modicum of methodology.

I have to admit that for all my intellectual disagreements with him I have been inspired by his empiricism and owe him a large share of my intellectual growth. I experienced a jump in my trading style in 1996, when Victor blurted to me that any "testable" statement should be *tested* (it was so obvious but I had not done it until then). His advice went straight home. A testable statement is one that can be broken down into quantitative components and subjected to statistical examination. For instance, a conventional-wisdom style statement like

accidents happen closer to home

can be tested by taking the average distance between the accident and the domicile of the driver (if, say, about 20% of accidents happen within a 12-mile radius). However, one needs to be careful in the interpretation; a naïve interpreter of the result would tell you that you are more likely to have an accident if you drive in your neighborhood than if you did so in remote places, which is an example of naïve empiricism. Why? Because accidents may happen closer to home simply because people spend their time driving close to home (if people spend 20% of their time driving in a 12-mile radius).

Since that very same day I have not made a single testable proposition without testing it, thanks to the computer which I rarely use for non-computational tasks. However, the differences between Victor Niederhoffer and myself remain immense; I can use data to disprove a proposition, never to prove one. I can use history to refute a conjecture, never to affirm it. For instance, the statement

The market never goes down 20% in a given 3-month period

can be tested, but is completely meaningless if verified. I can quantitatively reject the proposition by finding counterexamples, but it is impossible for me to accept it simply because in past data the market never went down 20% in any 3-month period.

Returning to the black swan problem, consider the following statement:

Statement A: No swan is black because I looked at 4000 swans and found none.
Statement B: Not all swans are white.

I cannot logically make statement A, no matter how many successive white swans I may have observed in my life and may observe in the future (except of course if I am given the privilege of observing with certainty all available swans). It is however possible to make Statement B merely by finding one single black swan in my sample. Indeed, statement A was disproved by the discovery of Australia, as it led to the sighting of the *cygnus atratus*, a swan variety that was jet black! The reader will see a hint of Popper (after we are done with my semi-mentor Victor); there is a strong asymmetry between the two statements. Such asymmetry lies in the foundations of knowledge. It is also at the core of my dealing with randomness as a trader.

The following inductive statement illustrates the problem of interpreting past data without logical *method*:

I have just completed a thorough statistical examination of the life of President Bush. For 55 years, close to 16,000 observations, he did not die once. I can hence pronounce him as immortal, with a high degree of statistical significance.

Although Victor and I trade in such an opposite manner that many of his trades end up in my inventory, I have a large measure of respect for him. He sells out-of-the-money options for a living; I buy them for a living (by selling an out-of-the-money option one is betting that an event *will not* happen; by buying one I am merely betting that it *may* happen). He tries to make steady income, I prefer a lumpy and rare payoff. Although we seem to be diametrically opposite traders, we share many superficial personal traits. These may be worth bringing in here because we both make our private traits part of our trading and make a thin distinction between activities middlebrow people call "work" and those they call "leisure". Both of us are traders trying to live under the illusion of operating a scientific laboratory. Both of us surround ourselves with scholars and scientists, not businessmen (talking to successful scientists is a good discipline to avoid pedestrianism in our own thinking). Both of us try to lead the lives of the Victorian gentleman scholar with books scattered around us, by escaping many of the popular accretions of the twentieth century. Both of us glorify our personal idiosyncrasies to avoid bearing any intellectual resemblance to the crowd. Both of us obsessively pursue athletic activities on a daily basis (but he is competitive and competition in sports repels me). Victor's model seems to be the Victorian gentleman (like his hero Francis Galton, the tinkering cousin of Charles Darwin, who is the true inspiration of all applied statisticians) while, like a true Victorian, I am first and last a classicist and remain steeped in the Greco-Roman culture in which I grew up (my heroes are rather literary figures). Both of us avoid the media, television, newspapers, although Victor is far more vigorous than I in such strictures. Both of us avoid chitchat and small talk like the plague (too much left-column noise).

Sir Karl's Promoting Agent

Next I will discuss how I discovered Karl Popper via another trader, perhaps the only one I have ever truly respected. I do not know if it applies to other people, but, in spite of my being a voracious reader, I have rarely been truly affected in my behavior (in any durable manner) by anything I have read. A book can make a strong impression, but such an impression tends to wane after some newer impression replaces it in my brain (a new book). I have to discover things by myself (recall *The Stove is Hot* section in Chapter 2). These self discoveries last.

One exception of ideas that stuck with me are those of Sir Karl, whom I discovered (or perhaps rediscovered) through the writings of the trader and self-styled philosopher George Soros who seemed to have organized his life by becoming a promoter of the ideas of Karl Popper. What I learned from George Soros was not quite in the way he perhaps intended us to learn from him. I disagreed with his statements when it came to economics and philosophy – but somehow I succumbed to the charm of this Hungarian man who like me is ashamed of being a trader and prefers his trading to be a minor extension of his intellectual life (it can be seen in his first book *The Alchemy of Finance*). Having never been impressed by people with money (and I have met plenty of those throughout my life), I did not look at any of them as remotely a role model for me. Perhaps the opposite effect holds, as I am generally repelled by the wealthy, generally because of the attitude of epic heroism that usually accompanies rapid enrichment. Soros was the only one who seemed to share my values. He wanted to be taken seriously as a Middle European professor who happened to have gotten rich owing to the validity of his ideas (it was only by failing to gain acceptance by other intellectuals that he would try to gain alpha status through his money, sort of like a seducer who after trying hard, would end up using such an appendage as the red Ferrari to seduce the girl). In addition, although Soros did not come across very clearly in his writings, he knew how to handle randomness, by keeping a critical open mind and changing his opinions with minimal shame (which carries the side effect of making him treat people like napkins). He walked around calling himself fallible, but was so potent because he knew it while others had loftier ideas about themselves. He understood Popper. He lived a Popperian life.

As an aside, Popper was not new to me. I had briefly heard of Karl Popper when I was in my teens and early twenties, as part of a motivated education in Europe and the United States. But I did not understand his ideas as presented then, nor did I think it would be important (like metaphysics) for anything in life. I was at the age when one felt like one needed to read everything, which prevented one from making contemplative stops. Such hurry made it hard to detect that there was something important in Popper. It was either my conditioning by the intellectual-chic culture at the time (too much Plato, too many Marxists, too much Hegel, too many pseudoscientific intellectuals), the educational system (too many conjectures propounded as truth) or the fact that I was too young and was reading too much then to make a bridge to reality.

Popper then slipped out of my mind without hanging on a single brain cell – there was nothing in the baggage of a boy without experience to let it stick. Besides, having started trading, I entered an anti-intellectual phase; I needed to make a non-random buck to secure my newly lost future and wealth that had just evaporated with the Lebanese war (until then I was living with the desire to become a comfortable man of leisure like almost everyone in my family, over the past two centuries). I suddenly felt financially insecure and feared becoming an employee of some firm that would turn me into a corporate slave with "work ethics" (whenever I hear *work ethics* I interpret *inefficient mediocrity*). I needed the backing of my bank account so I could buy time to think and enjoy life. The last thing I needed was immediate philosophizing and work at the local McDonald's. Philosophy, to me, became something rhetorical people did when they had plenty of time on their hands; it was an activity reserved to those who are not well versed in quantitative methods and other productive things. It was a pastime that should be limited to late hours, in bars around the campuses, when one had a few drinks and a light schedule – provided one forgot the garrulous episode as early as the next day. Too much of it can get a man in trouble, perhaps turn one into a Marxist ideologue. Popper was not to reemerge until I secured my career as a trader.

LOCATION, LOCATION

It is said that people generally remember the time and geographic condition where they were swept with a governing idea. The religious poet and diplomat Paul Claudel remembers the exact spot of his *conversion* (or re-conversion) to Catholicism in the Cathedral Notre-Dame of Paris, near a precise column. Thus I remember exactly the spot at Barnes and Noble on 21st Street and Fifth Avenue where in 1987, inspired by Soros, I read 50 pages of *The Logic of Scientific Discovery* and feverishly bought all the Popper titles I could get my hands on lest they run out of stock. It was in a sparsely lit side-room that had a distinctive smell of mildew. I remember vividly the thoughts that rushed through my head like a revelation.

Popper turned out to be exactly the opposite of what I initially thought about "philosophers"; he was the epitome of no nonsense. By then I had been an option trader for a couple of years and I felt angry that I was being taken for a total ride by the academic researchers in finance, particularly since I was deriving my income from the failure of their models. I had already started talking to finance academics as part of my involvement with derivatives and I had trouble getting through to them some basic points about financial markets (they believed in their models a little too much). There was all along lurking in my mind the idea that these researchers had missed a point, but I did not quite know what it was. It was not what they knew, it was *how* they knew it that was the subject of my annoyance.

POPPER'S ANSWER

Popper came up with a major answer to the problem of induction (to me he came up with *the* answer). No man has influenced the way scientists do science more than Sir Karl – in spite of the fact that many of his fellow professional philosophers find him quite naïve (to his credit, in my opinion). Popper's idea is that science is not to be taken as seriously as it sounds (Popper when meeting Einstein did not take him as the demigod he thought he was). There are only two types of theories:

1. Theories that are known to be wrong, as they were tested and adequately rejected (he calls them *falsified*).
2. Theories that have not yet been known to be wrong, not *falsified* yet, but are exposed to be proved wrong.

Why is a theory never *right*? Because we will never know if all the swans are white (Popper borrowed the Kantian idea of the flaws in our mechanisms of perception). The testing mechanism may be faulty. However, the statement that there is a black swan is possible to make. A theory cannot be *verified*. To paraphrase baseball coach Yogi Berra again, *past data has a lot of good in it, but it is the bad side that is bad*. It can only be provisionally accepted. A theory that falls outside of these two categories is not a theory. A theory that does not present a set of conditions under which it would be considered wrong would be termed charlatanism – they would be impossible to reject otherwise. Why? Because the astrologist can always find a reason to fit the past event, by saying that *Mars was probably in line but not too much so* (likewise to me a trader who does not have a point that would make him change his mind is not a trader). Indeed the difference between Newtonian physics, which was falsified by Einstein's relativity, and astrology lies in the following irony. Newtonian physics is scientific because it allowed us to falsify it, as we know that it is wrong, while astrology is not because it does not offer conditions under which we could reject it. Astrology cannot be disproved, owing to the auxiliary hypotheses that come into play. Such point lies at the basis of the demarcation between science and nonsense (called "the problem of demarcation").

More practically to me, Popper had many problems with statistics and statisticians. He refused to blindly accept the notion that knowledge can always increase with incremental information – which is the foundation of statistical inference. It may in some instances, but we do not know which ones. Many insightful people, such as John Maynard Keynes, independently reached the same conclusions. Sir Karl's detractors believe that favorably repeating the same experiment again and again should lead to an increased comfort with the notion that "it works". I came to understand Popper's position better once I saw the first rare event ravaging a trading room. Sir Karl feared that some type of knowledge did not increase with information – but which type we could not ascertain. The reason I feel that he is important for us traders is because to him the matter of knowledge and discovery is not so much in dealing with what we know, as in dealing with what we do not know. His famous quote:

> *These are men with bold ideas, but highly critical of their own ideas; they try to find whether their ideas are right by trying first to find whether they are not perhaps wrong. They work with bold conjectures and severe attempts at refuting their own conjectures.*

"These" are scientists. But they could be anything.

Putting the master in context, Popper was rebelling against the growth of science. Popper intellectually came to the world with the dramatic shifts in philosophy as attempts were made to shift it from the verbal and rhetorical to the scientific and rigorous, as we saw with the presentation of the Vienna Circle in Chapter 4. These people were sometimes called the logical positivists, after the movement called *positivism* pioneered in France in the nineteenth century by Auguste Comte, where positivism meant scientification of things (literally everything under the sun). It was the equivalent of bringing the industrial revolution into the soft sciences.

Without dwelling on positivism, I have to note that Popper is the antidote to positivism. To him, verification is not possible. Verificationism is more dangerous than anything else. Taken to the extreme, Popper's ideas appear naïve and primitive – but they work. Note that his detractors call him a *naïve falsificationist*.

I am an exceedingly naïve falsificationist. Why? Because I can survive being one. My extreme and obsessive Popperism is carried out as follows. I speculate in all of my activities on theories that represent some vision of the world, but with the following stipulation: no rare event should harm me. In fact, I would like all conceivable rare events to help me. My idea of science diverges with that of the people around me walking around calling themselves scientists. Science is mere speculation, mere formulation of conjecture.

OPEN SOCIETY

Popper's falsificationism is intimately connected to the notion of an open society. An open society is one in which no permanent truth is held to exist; this would allow counterideas to emerge. Karl Popper shared ideas with his friend, the low-key economist Von Hayek who endorsed capitalism as a state in which prices can disseminate information that bureaucratic socialism would choke. Both notions of falsificationism and open society are, counterintuitively, connected to those of a rigorous method for handling randomness in my day job as a trader. Clearly, an open mind is a necessity when dealing with randomness. Popper believed that any idea of Utopia is necessarily closed in the fact that it chokes its own refutations. The simple notion of a good model for society that cannot be left open for falsification is totalitarian. I learned from Popper, in addition to the difference between an open and a closed society, that between an open and a closed mind.

NOBODY IS PERFECT

I have some sobering information about Popper the man. Witnesses of his private life find him rather un-Popperian. The philosopher and

Oxford don Brian Magee[6] who befriended him for close to three decades depicts him as unworldly (except in his youth) and narrowly focused on his work. He spent the last 50 years of his long career (Popper lived 92 years) closed to the outside world, insulated from outside distractions and stimulation. Popper also engaged in giving people "firm sounding advice about their career or their private life, though he had little understanding of either. All this, of course, was in direct contravention of his professed (and indeed genuine) beliefs, and practices, in philosophy."

He was not much better in his youth. Members of the Vienna Circle tried to avoid him, not because of his divergent ideas, but because he was a social problem. "He was brilliant, but self-focused, both insecure and arrogant, irascible and self-righteous. He was a terrible listener and bent on winning arguments at all costs. He had no understanding of group dynamics and no ability to negotiate them".[7]

I will refrain from commonplace discourse about the divorce between those who have ideas and those who carry them in practice, except to bring out the interesting genetics problem; we like to emit logical and rational ideas but we do not necessarily *enjoy* this execution. Strange as it sounds, this point has only been discovered very recently (we will see that we are not genetically fit to be rational and act rationally; we are merely fit for the maximum probability of transmitting our genes in some given unsophisticated environment). Also strange as it sounds, George Soros, obsessively self-critical, seems to be more Popperian than Popper in his professional behavior.

PASCAL'S WAGER

I conclude with the exposition of my own method of dealing with the problem of induction. The philosopher Pascal proclaimed that the optimal strategy for humans is to believe in the existence of God. For if God exists, then the believer would be rewarded. If he does not exist, the believer would have nothing to lose. Accordingly, we need to accept the asymmetry in knowledge; there are situations in which using statistics and econometrics can be useful. But I do not want my life to depend on it.

Like Pascal, I will therefore state the following argument. If the science of statistics can benefit me in anything, I will use it. If it poses a threat, then I will not. I want to take the best of what the past can give me without its dangers. Accordingly, I will use statistics and inductive methods to make aggressive bets, but I will not use them to manage my risks and exposure. Surprisingly, all the surviving traders I know seem to have done the same. They trade on ideas based on some observation (that includes past history) but, like the Popperian scientists, they make sure that the costs of being wrong are limited (and their probability is not derived from past data). Unlike Carlos and John, they know before getting involved in the trading strategy which events would prove their conjecture wrong and allow for it (recall that Carlos and John used past history both to make their bets and measure their risk). They would then terminate their trade. This is called a *stop loss*, a predetermined exit point, a protection from the black swan. I find it rarely practiced.

Thank You Solon

Finally, I have to confess that upon finishing my writing of Part I that writing about the genius of Solon's insight has carried an extreme effect on both my thinking and my private life. The composition of Part I made me even more confident in my withdrawal from the media and my distancing myself from other members of the business community, mostly other investors and traders for whom I am developing more and more contempt. I am currently enjoying a thrill of the classics I have not felt since childhood. My mind, by escaping the news pollution, allowed me to evade the bull market that prevailed over the past 15 years (and professionally benefit from its demise). I am now thinking of the next step: to recreate a low-information, more deterministic ancient time, say in the nineteenth century, all the while benefiting from some of the technical gains (such as the Monte Carlo engine), all of the medical breakthroughs and all the gains of social justice of our age. I would then have the best of everything. This is called evolution.

PART II

MONKEYS ON TYPEWRITERS - SURVIVORSHIP AND OTHER BIASES

I f one puts an infinite number of monkeys in front of (strongly built)
typewriters, and lets them clap away, there is a certainty that one of
them would come out with an exact version of the *Iliad*. Upon
examination, this may be less interesting a concept than it appears at
first: such probability is very low. But let us carry the reasoning one step
beyond. Now that we have found that hero among monkeys, would any
reader invest his life's savings on a bet that the monkey would write the
Odyssey next?

In this story, it is the second step that is interesting. How much can
past performance (here the typing of the *Iliad*) be relevant in forecasting
future performance? The same applies to any decision based on past
performance, merely relying on the attributes of the past time series.
Think about the monkey showing up at your door with his impressive
past performance. Hey, he wrote the *Iliad*. Quickly, sign him up for the
sequel.

The major problem with inference in general is that those whose
profession is to derive conclusions from data often fall into the trap
faster and more confidently than others. The more data we have, the
more likely we are to drown in it. For common wisdom among people
with a budding knowledge of probability laws is to base their decision-
making on the following principle: it is very unlikely for someone to

perform considerably well in a consistent fashion without his doing something right. Track records therefore become preeminent. They call on the rule of the likelihood of such a successful run and tell themselves that if someone performed better than the rest in the past then there is a great chance of him performing better than the crowd in the future – and a very great one at that. But, as usual, beware the middlebrow: a small knowledge of probability can lead to worse results than no knowledge at all.

IT DEPENDS ON THE NUMBER OF MONKEYS

I do not deny that if someone performed better than the crowd in the past, there is a presumption of his ability to do better in the future. But the presumption might be weak, very weak, to the point of being useless in decision making. Why? Because it all depends on two factors: the randomness content of his profession and the number of monkeys in operation.

The initial sample size matters greatly. If there are five monkeys in the game, I would be rather impressed with the *Iliad* writer, to the point of suspecting him to be a reincarnation of the ancient poet. If there are a billion to the power one billion monkeys I would be less impressed – as a matter of fact I would be surprised if one of them did not get some well known (but unspecified) piece of work, just by luck (perhaps Casanova's *Memoirs of My Life*). One monkey would even be expected to provide us with former Vice President Al Gore's *Earth in the Balance*, perhaps stripped of the platitudes.

This problem enters the business world more viciously than other walks of life, owing to the high dependence on randomness (we have already belabored the contrast between randomness-dependent business with dentistry). The greater the number of businessmen, the greater the likelihood of one of them performing in a stellar manner just by luck. I have rarely seen anyone count the monkeys. In the same vein, few count the investors in the market in order to calculate, instead of the probability of success, the conditional probability of successful runs given the number of investors in operation over a given market history.

VICIOUS REAL LIFE

There are other aspects to the monkeys problem; in real life the other monkeys are not countable, let alone visible. They are hidden away, as one sees only the winners – it is natural for those who failed to vanish completely. Accordingly, one sees the survivors, and only the survivors, which imparts such a mistaken perception of the odds. We do not respond to probability, but to society's assessment of it. As we saw with Nero Tulip, even people with training in probability respond unintelligently to social pressure.

THIS SECTION

Part I described situations where people do not understand the rare event, and do not seem to accept either the possibility of its occurrence or the dire consequences of such occurrence. It also set out my own ideas, those that do not seem to have been explored in the literature. But a book on randomness is not complete without a presentation of what possible biases one might have aside from the deformations caused by the rare event. The business of Part II is more pedestrian; I will rapidly provide a synthesis of the biases of randomness as discussed in the now abundant literature on the subject.

These biases can be outlined as follows: (a) the survivorship biases (a.k.a. monkeys on a typewriter), arising from the fact that we see only winners and get a distorted view of the odds (Chapters 8 and 9, *Too Many Millionaires* and *Fry an Egg*), (b) the fact that luck is most frequently the reason for extreme success (Chapter 10, *Loser Takes All*), and (c) the biological handicap of our inability to understand probability (Chapter 11, *Randomness and Our Brain*).

EIGHT

TOO MANY MILLIONAIRES NEXT DOOR

Three illustrations of the survivorship bias. Why very few people should live on Park Avenue. The millionaire next door has very flimsy clothes. An overcrowding of experts.

How To Stop the Sting of Failure

SOMEWHAT HAPPY

Marc lives on Park Avenue in New York City with his wife Janet and their three children. He makes $500,000 a year, give or take a boom or a recession – he does not believe that the recent spurt in prosperity is here to last and has not mentally adjusted yet to his recent abrupt rise in income. A rotund man in his late forties, with spongy features that make him look ten years older than his age, he leads the seemingly comfortable (but heckled) life of a New York city lawyer. But he is on the quiet side of Manhattan residents. Marc is clearly not the man one would expect to go bar-hopping or attend late night Tribecca and Soho parties. He and his wife have a country house and a rose garden and tend to be concerned, like many people of their age, mentality, and condition, with (in the following order) material comfort, health, and status. Weekdays, he does not come home until at least 9.30 p.m. and, at times, he can be found in the office at close to midnight. By the end of the week, Marc is so fatigued that he falls asleep during their three-hour drive to "the house"; and Marc spends most of Saturday lying in bed recovering and healing.

Marc grew up in a small town in the midwest, the son of a quiet tax accountant who worked with sharp yellow pencils. His obsession with sharpness was so strong that he carried a sharpener in his pocket at all times. Marc exhibited very early signs of intelligence. He did extremely well in high school. He attended Harvard College, then Yale Law School. Not bad, one would say. Later his career took him to corporate law, where he started working on large cases for a prestigious New York law firm, with barely enough hours left for him to brush his teeth. This is not too much an exaggeration, for he ate almost all of his dinners in the office, accumulating body fat and Brownie points towards his partnership. He later became a partner within the usual seven years, but not without the usual human costs. His first wife (whom he met in college) left him, as she was tired of an absentee lawyer husband and weary of the deterioration in his conversation – but, ironically, she ended up moving in with and later marrying another New York lawyer, probably with a no-less flat conversation, but who made her happier.

TOO MUCH WORK

Marc's body became progressively flabbier, and his tailored suits needed periodic visits to the tailor, in spite of his occasional crash diets. After he got over the depression of the abandonment, he started dating Janet, his paralegal, and promptly married her. They had three children in quick succession, bought the Park Avenue apartment, and the country house.

Janet's immediate acquaintance is composed of the other parents of the Manhattan private school attended by their children, and their neighbors at the co-operative apartment building where they live. From a materialistic standpoint, they come at the low end of such a set, perhaps even at the exact bottom. They would be the poorest of these circles, as their co-op is inhabited by extremely successful corporate executives, Wall Street traders, and high-flying entrepreneurs. Their children's private school harbors the second set of children of corporate raiders, from their trophy wives – perhaps even the third set, if one takes into account the age discrepancy and the model-like features of the other mothers. By comparison, Marc's wife Janet, like him, presents a homely country-home-with-a-rose-garden type of appearance.

YOU'RE A FAILURE

Marc's strategy of staying in Manhattan may be rational, as his demanding work hours would make it impossible for him to commute. But the costs on his wife Janet are monstrous. Why? Because of their relative nonsuccess – as geographically defined by their Park Avenue neighborhood. Every month or so, Janet has a crisis, giving in to the strains and humiliations of being snubbed by some other mother at the school where she picks up the children, or another woman with larger diamonds by the elevator of the co-op where they live in the smallest type of apartments (the G line). Why isn't her husband so successful? Isn't he smart and hard working? Didn't he get close to 1600 at the SAT? Why is this Ronald Something whose wife never even nods to Janet, worth hundred of millions when her husband went to Harvard and Yale and has such a high I.Q., and has hardly any substantial savings?

We will not get too involved in the Chekovian dilemmas in the private lives of Marc and Janet, but their case provides a very common illustration of the emotional effect of *survivorship bias*. Janet feels that her husband is a failure, by comparison, but she is mis-computing the probabilities in a gross manner – she is using the wrong distribution to derive a rank. As compared to the general U.S. population, Marc has done very well, better than 99.5% of his compatriots. As compared to his high-school friends, he did extremely well, a fact that he could have verified had he had time to attend the periodic reunions, and he would come at the top. As compared to the other people at Harvard, he did better than 90% of them (financially, of course). As compared to his law school comrades at Yale, he did better than 60% of them. But as compared to his co-op neighbors, he is at the bottom! Why? Because he chose to live among the people who have been successful, in an area that excludes failure. In other words, those who have failed do not show up in the sample at all, thus making him look as if he were not doing well at all. By living on Park Avenue, one does not have exposure to the losers, one only sees the winners. As we are cut to live in very small communities, it is difficult to assess our situation outside of the narrowly defined geographic confines of our habitat. In the case of Marc and Janet, this leads to considerable emotional distress; here we have a woman who married an extremely successful man but all she can see is comparative failure, for she cannot emotionally compare him to a sample that would do him justice.

Someone would rationally say to Janet: "go read this book, *Fooled by Randomness* by one mathematical trader on the deformations of chance in life; it would give you a statistical sense of perspective and would accordingly make you feel better". As an author, I would like to offer a panacea for $27.95, but I would rather say that in my best hopes it may provide an hour or so of solace. Janet may need something more drastic for relief. I have repeated that becoming more rational, or not feeling emotions of social slights is not part of the human race, at least not with our current DNA code. There is no solace to be found from reasoning – as a trader I have learned something about these unfruitful efforts to reason against the grain. I would advise Janet to move out, and go live in some blue-collar neighborhood where they would feel less humiliated by their neighbors and rise in the pecking order beyond their probability of success. They could use the deformation in the opposite direction. If Janet cares about status, then I would even recommend some of these large housing blocks.

Double Survivorship Biases

MORE EXPERTS

I recently read a bestseller called *The Millionaire Next Door*, an extremely misleading (but almost enjoyable) book by two "experts", in which the authors try to infer some attributes that are common to rich people. They examined a collection of currently wealthy people and found out that these are unlikely to lead lavish lives. They call such people the accumulators; persons ready to postpone consumption in order to amass funds. Most of the appeal of the book comes from the simple but counterintuitive fact that these are less likely to look like very rich people – it clearly costs money to look and behave rich, not to count the time demands of spending money. Leading prosperous lives is time consuming; shopping for trendy clothes, becoming conversant in Bordeaux wines, getting to know the expensive restaurants. All these activities can put high demands on one's time and divert the subject from what should be the real preoccupation, namely the accumulation of nominal (and paper) wealth. The moral of the book is that the wealthiest are to be found among those less suspected to be wealthy. On the other hand, those who act and look wealthy subject their net worth to such a drain that they inflict considerable and irreversible damage to their brokerage account.

I will set aside the point that I see no special *heroism* in accumulating money, particularly if, in addition, the person is foolish enough to not even try to derive any tangible benefit from the wealth (aside from the pleasure of regularly counting the beans). I have no large desire to sacrifice much of my personal habits, intellectual pleasures, and personal standards in order to become a billionaire like Warren Buffett, and I certainly do not see the point of becoming one if I were to adopt Spartan (even miserly) habits and live in my starter house. Something about the praise lavished upon him for living in austerity while being so rich escapes me; if austerity is the end, he should become a monk or a social worker – we should remember that becoming rich is a purely selfish act, not a social one. The virtue of capitalism is that society can take advantage of people's greed rather than their benevolence, but there is no need to, in addition, extol such greed as a moral (or intellectual) accomplishment (the reader can easily see that, aside from very few exceptions like George Soros, I am not impressed by people with money). Becoming rich is not directly a moral achievement, but that is not where the severe flaw in the book lies.

As we said, the heroes of *The Millionaire Next Door* are the accumulators, people who defer spending in order to invest. It is undeniable that such strategy might work; money spent bears no fruit (except the enjoyment of the spender). But the benefits promised in the book seem grossly overstated. A finer read of their thesis reveals that their sample includes a double dose of survivorship bias. In other words, it has two compounding flaws.

VISIBILITY WINNERS

The first bias comes from the fact that the rich people selected for their sample are among the lucky monkeys on typewriters. The authors made no attempt to correct their statistics with the fact that they saw only the winners. They make no mention of the "accumulators" who have accumulated the wrong things (members of my family are experts on that; those who accumulated managed to accumulate currencies about to be devalued and stocks of companies that later went bust). Nowhere do we see a mention of the fact that some people were lucky enough to have invested in the winners; these people no doubt would make their way into the book. There is a way to take care of the bias: lower the wealth of your average millionaire by, say, 50%, on the grounds that the bias causes the average net worth of the observed millionaire to be higher by such amount (it consists in adding the effect of the losers into the pot). It would certainly modify the conclusion.

IT'S A BULL MARKET

As to the second, more serious flaw, I have already discussed the problem of induction. The story focuses on an unusual episode in history; buying its thesis implies accepting that the current returns in asset values are permanent (the sort of belief that prevailed before the great crash that started in 1929). Remember that asset prices have (still at the time of writing) witnessed the greatest bull market in history and that values did compound astronomically during the past two decades. A dollar invested in the average stock would have grown almost twenty-fold since 1982 – and that is the average stock. The sample might include people who invested in stocks performing better than average.

Virtually all of the subjects became rich from asset price inflation, in other words from the recent inflation in financial paper and assets that started in 1982. An investor who engaged in the same strategy during less august days for the market would certainly have a different story to tell. Imagine the book being written in 1982, after the prolonged erosion of the inflation-adjusted value of the stocks, or in 1935, after the loss of interest in the stock market.

Or consider that the United States stock market is not the only investment vehicle. Consider the fate of those who, in place of spending their money buying expensive toys and paying for ski trips, bought Lebanese lira denominated Treasury bills (as my grandfather did), or junk bonds from Michael Milken (as many of my colleagues in the 1980s did). Go back in history and imagine the accumulator buying Russian Imperial bonds bearing the signature of Czar Nicholas II and trying to accumulate further by cashing them from the Soviet government, or Argentine real estate in the 1930s (as my great grandfather did).

The mistake of ignoring the survivorship bias is chronic, even (or perhaps especially) among professionals. How? Because we are trained to take advantage of the information that is lying in front of our eyes, ignoring the information that we do not see.

A brief summing up at this point: I showed how we tend to mistake one realization among all possible random histories as the most representative one, forgetting that there may be others. In a nutshell, the survivorship bias implies that *the highest performing realization will be the most visible*. Why? Because the losers do not show up.

A Guru's Opinion

The fund management industry is populated with gurus. Clearly, the field is randomness-laden and the guru is going to fall into a trap, particularly if he has no proper training in inference. At the time of writing, there is one such guru who developed the very unfortunate habit of writing books on the subject. Along with one of his peers, he computed the success of a "Robin Hood" policy of investing with the least successful manager in a given population of managers. It consists in switching down by taking money away from the winner and allocating it to the loser. This goes against the prevailing wisdom of investing with a winning manager and taking away money from a losing one. Doing so, their "paper strategy" (i.e. as in a Monopoly™ game, not executed in real life) derived considerably higher returns than if they stuck to the winning manager. Their hypothetical example seemed to them to prove that one should not stay with the best manager, as we would be inclined to do, but rather switch to the worst manager, or at least such seems to be the point they were attempting to convey.

Their analysis presents one severe hitch that any graduate student in financial economics should be able to pinpoint at the first reading. Their sample only had *survivors*. They simply forgot to take into account the managers who went out of business. Such a sample includes managers that were operating during the simulation, and *are still operating today*. True, their sample included managers who did poorly, but only those managers who did poorly and recovered, without getting out of business. So it would be obvious that investing with those who fared poorly at some point, but recovered (with the benefit of hindsight) would yield a positive return! Had they continued to fare poorly, they would be out of business and would not be included in the sample.

How should one conduct the proper simulation? By taking a population of managers in existence, say, five years ago and running the simulation until today. Clearly, the attributes of those who leave the population are biased towards failure; few successful people in such a lucrative business call it quits for making too much money. Next we turn to a more technical presentation of these issues.

NINE

$$\maltese$$

IT IS EASIER TO BUY AND SELL THAN FRY AN EGG

Some technical extensions of the survivorship bias. On the distribution of "coincidences" in life. It is preferable to be lucky than competent (but you can be caught). The birthday paradox. More charlatans (and more journalists). How the researcher with work ethics can find just about anything in data. On dogs not barking.

This afternoon I have an appointment with my dentist (it will mostly consist in the dentist picking my brain on Brazilian bonds). I can state with a certain level of comfort that he knows something about teeth, particularly if I enter his office with a toothache and exit it with some form of relief. It will be difficult for someone who knows literally nothing about teeth to provide me with such relief, except if he is particularly lucky on that day – or has been very lucky in his life to become a dentist while not knowing anything about teeth. Looking at his diploma on the wall, I determine that the odds that he repeatedly gave correct answers to the exam questions and performed satisfactorily on a few thousand cavities before his graduation – out of plain randomness – are remarkably small.

Later in the evening, I go to Carnegie Hall. I can say little about the pianist; I even forgot her unfamiliar foreign sounding name. All I know is that she studied in some Muscovite conservatory. But I can expect to get some music out of the piano. It will be rare to have someone who performed brilliantly enough in the past to get to Carnegie Hall and now turns out to have benefited from luck alone. The expectation of having a fraud who will bang on the piano, producing only cacophonous sounds, is indeed low enough for me to rule it out completely.

I was in London last Saturday. Saturdays in London are magical; bustling but without the mechanical industry of a weekday or the sad resignation of a Sunday. Without a wristwatch or a plan I found myself in front of my favorite carvings by Canova at the Victoria and Albert Museum. My professional bent immediately made me question whether randomness played a large role in the carving of these marble statues. The bodies were realistic reproductions of human figures, except that they were more harmonious and finely balanced than anything I have seen mother nature produce on its own (Ovid's *materiem superabat opus* comes to mind). Could such finesse be a product of luck?

I can practically make the same statement about anyone operating in the physical world, or in a business in which the degree of randomness is low. But there is a problem in anything related to the business world. I am bothered because tomorrow, unfortunately, I have an appointment with a fund manager seeking my help, and that of my friends, in finding investors. He has what he claims is a *good track record*. All I can infer is that he has learned to buy and sell. And it is harder to fry an egg than buy and sell. Well ... the fact that he made money in the past may have some relevance, but not terribly so. This is not to say that it is always the case; there are some instances in which one can trust a track record, but, alas, there are not too many of these. As the reader now knows, the fund manager can expect to be heckled by me during the presentation, particularly if he does not exhibit the minimum of humility and self-doubt that I would expect from someone practicing randomness. I will probably bombard him with questions that he may not be prepared to answer, blinded by his past results. I will probably lecture him that Machiavelli ascribed to luck at least a 50% role in life (the rest was cunning and bravura), and that was before the creation of modern markets.

In this chapter, I discuss some well-known counterintuitive properties of performance records and historical time series. The concept presented here is well known for some of its variations under the name *survivorship bias*, *data mining*, *data snooping*, *overfitting*, *regression to the mean*, etc., basically situations where the performance is exaggerated by the observer, owing to a misperception of the importance of randomness. Clearly, this concept has rather unsettling implications. It extends to more general situations where randomness may play a share, such as the choice of a medical treatment or the interpretation of coincidental events.

When I am tempted to suggest a possible future contribution of financial research to science in general, I adduce the analysis of data mining and the study of survivorship biases. These have been refined in finance but can extend to all areas of scientific investigation. Why is finance so rich a field? Because it is one of the rare areas of investigation where we have plenty of information (in the form of abundant price series), but no ability to conduct experiments as in, say, physics. This dependence on past data brings about its salient defects.

Fooled by Numbers

PLACEBO INVESTORS

I have often been faced with questions of the sort: "Who do you think you are to tell me that I might have been plain lucky in my life?" Well, nobody really believes that he or she was lucky. My approach is that, with our Monte Carlo engine, we can manufacture purely random situations. We can do the exact opposite of conventional methods; in place of analyzing real people hunting for attributes we can create artificial ones with precisely known attributes. Thus we can manufacture situations that depend on pure, unadulterated luck, without the shadow of skills or whatever we have called non-luck in Table P.1. In other words, we can man-make pure nobodies to laugh at; they will be *by design* stripped of any shadow of ability (exactly like a placebo drug).

We saw in Chapter 5 how people may survive owing to traits that momentarily fit the given structure of randomness. Here we take a far simpler situation where *we know the structure of randomness*; the first such exercise is a finessing of the old popular saying that *even a broken clock is right twice a day*. We will take it a bit further to show that statistics is a knife that cuts on both sides. Let us use the Monte Carlo generator introduced earlier and construct a population of 10,000 fictional investment managers (the generator is not terribly necessary since we can use a coin, or even do plain algebra, but it is considerably more illustrative – and fun). Assume that they each have a perfectly fair game; each one has a 50% probability of making $10,000 at the end of the year, and a 50% probability of losing $10,000. Let us introduce an additional restriction; once a manager has a single bad year, he is thrown out of the sample, good-bye and have a nice life. Thus we will operate like the legendary speculator George Soros who was said to tell his managers gathered in a room: "half of you guys will be out by next year" (with an Eastern European accent). Like Soros, we have extremely high standards; we are looking only for managers with an unblemished record. We have no patience for low performers.

The Monte Carlo generator will toss a coin; *heads* and the manager will make $10,000 over the year, *tails* and he will lose $10,000. We run it for the first year. At the end of the year, we expect 5,000 managers to be up $10,000 each, and 5,000 to be down $10,000. Now we run the game a second year. Again, we can expect 2,500 managers to be up two years in a row; another year, 1,250; a fourth one, 625; a fifth, 313. We have now, simply in a fair game, 313 managers who made money for five years in a row. Out of pure luck.

NOBODY HAS TO BE COMPETENT

Let's push the argument further to make it more interesting. We create a cohort that is composed exclusively of incompetent managers. We will define an incompetent manager as someone who has a negative *expected return*, the equivalent of the odds being stacked against him. We instruct the Monte Carlo generator now to draw from an urn. The urn has 100 balls, 45 black and 55 red. By drawing with replacement, the ratio of red to black balls will remain the same. If we draw a black ball, the manager will earn $10,000. If we draw a red ball, he will lose $10,000. The manager is thus expected to earn $10,000 with 45% probability, and lose $10,000 with 55%. On average, the manager will lose $1,000 each round – but only *on average*.

At the end of the first year, we still expect to have 4,500 managers turning a profit (45% of them), the second, 45% of that number, 2,025. The third, 911; the fourth, 410; the fifth, 184. Let us give the surviving managers names and dress them in business suits. True, they represent less than 2% of the original cohort. But they will get attention. Nobody will mention the other 98%. What can we conclude?

The first counterintuitive point is that a population entirely composed of bad managers will produce a small amount of great track records. As a matter of fact, assuming the manager shows up unsolicited at your door, it will be practically impossible to figure out whether he is good or bad. The results would not markedly change, even if the population were composed entirely of managers who are expected in the long run to lose money. Why? Because owing to volatility, some of them will make money. We can see here that volatility actually helps bad investment decisions.

The second counterintuitive point is that the *expectation of the maximum* of track records, with which we are concerned, depends more on the size of the initial sample, than on the individual odds per manager. In other words the number of managers with great track records in a given market depends far more on the number of people who started in the investment business (in place of going to dental school), rather than on their ability to produce profits. It also depends on the volatility. Why do I use the notion of expectation of the maximum? Because I am not concerned at all with the average track record. I will get to see only the *best* of the managers, not all of the managers. This means that we will see more "excellent managers" in 2002 than in 1998, provided the cohort of beginners was greater in 1997 than it was in 1993 – I can safely say that it was.

ERGODICITY

To get more technical, I have to say that people believe that they can figure out the properties of the distribution from the sample they are witnessing. When it comes to matters that depend on the maximum, it is altogether another distribution that is being inferred, that of the best performers. We call the difference between the average of such distribution and the unconditional distribution of winners and losers the *survivorship bias* – here the fact that about 3% of the initial cohort will make money five years in a row. In addition, this example illustrates the properties of *ergodicity*, namely, that time will eliminate the annoying effects of randomness. Looking forward, in spite of the fact that these managers were profitable in the past five years, we expect them to break even in any future time period. They will fare no better than those of the initial cohort who failed earlier in the exercise. Ah, the long term.

A few years ago, when I told one A., a then Master-of-the-Universe type, that track records were less relevant than he thought, he found the remark so offensive that he violently flung his cigarette lighter in my direction. The episode taught me a lot. Remember that nobody accepts randomness in his own success, only his failure. His ego was pumped up as he was heading up a department of "great traders" who were then temporarily making a fortune in the markets. They subsequently blew up during the harsh New York winter of 1994 (it was the bond market crash that followed the surprise interest rate hike by Alan Greenspan). The interesting part is that six years later I can hardly find any of them still trading (ergodicity).

Recall that the survivorship bias depends on the size of the initial population. The information that a person made money in the past, just by itself, is neither meaningful nor relevant. We need to know the size of the population from which he came. In other words, without knowing how many managers out there have tried and failed, we will not be able to assess the validity of the track record. If the initial population includes ten managers, then I would give the performer half my savings without a blink. If the initial population is composed of 10,000 managers, I would ignore the results. The latter situation is generally the case; these days so many people have been drawn to the financial markets. Many college graduates are trading as a first career, failing, then going to dental school.

If, as in a fairy tale, these fictional managers materialized into real human beings, one of these could be the person I am meeting tomorrow at 11.45 a.m. Why did I select 11.45 a.m.? Because I will question him about his trading style. I need to know how he trades. I will then be able to claim that I have to rush to a lunch appointment if the manager puts too much emphasis on his track record.

Life Is Coincidental

Next we look at the extensions to real life of our bias in the understanding of the distribution of coincidences.

THE MYSTERIOUS LETTER

You get an anonymous letter on January 2nd informing you that the market will go up during the month. It proves to be true, but you disregard it owing to the well-known January effect (stocks have gone up historically during January). Then you receive another one on Feb 1st telling you that the market will go down. Again, it proves to be true. Then you get another letter on March 1st – same story. By July you are intrigued by the prescience of the anonymous person and you are asked to invest in a special offshore fund. You pour all your savings into it. Two months later, your money is gone. You go spill your tears on your neighbor's shoulder and he tells you that he remembers that he received two such mysterious letters. But the mailings stopped at the second letter. He recalls that the first one was correct in its prediction, the other incorrect.

What happened? The trick is as follows. The con operator pulls 10,000 names out of a phone book. He mails a bullish letter to one half of the sample, and a bearish one to the other half. The following month he selects the names of the persons to whom he mailed the letter whose prediction turned out to be right, that is, 5,000 names. The next month he does the same with the remaining 2,500 names, until the list narrows down to 500 people. Of these there will be 200 victims. An investment in a few thousand dollars worth of postage stamps will turn into several million.

AN INTERRUPTED TENNIS GAME

It is not uncommon for someone watching a tennis game on television to be bombarded by advertisements for funds that did (until that minute) outperform others by some percentage over some period. But, again, why would anybody advertise if he didn't happen to outperform the market? There is a high probability of the investment coming to you if its success is caused entirely by randomness. This phenomenon is what economists and insurance people call adverse selection. Judging an investment that comes to you requires more stringent standards than judging an investment you seek, owing to such selection bias. For example, by going to a cohort composed of 10,000 managers, I have 2/ 100 chances of finding a spurious survivor. By staying home and answering my door bell, the chance of the soliciting party being a spurious survivor is closer to 100%.

THE BIRTHDAY PARADOX

The most intuitive way to describe the data mining problem to a non-statistician is through what is called the birthday paradox, though it is not really a paradox, simply a perceptional oddity. If you meet someone randomly, there is a one in 365.25 chance of your sharing their birthday, and a considerably smaller one of having the exact birthday of the same year. So, sharing the same birthday would be a coincidental event that you would discuss at the dinner table. Now let us look at a situation where there are 23 people in a room. What is the chance of there being two people with the same birthday? About 50%. For we are not specifying which people need to share a birthday; any pair works.

IT'S A SMALL WORLD!

A similar misconception of probabilities arises from the random encounters one may have with relatives or friends in highly unexpected places. "It's a small world" is often uttered with surprise. But these are not improbable occurrences – the world is much larger than we think. It is just that we are not truly testing for the odds of having an encounter with one specific person, in a specific location at a specific time. Rather, we are simply testing for any encounter, with any person we have ever met in the past, and in any place we will visit during the period concerned. The probability of the latter is considerably higher, perhaps several thousand times the magnitude of the former.

When the statistician looks at the data *to test a given relationship*, say to ferret out the correlation between the occurrence of a given event, like a political announcement, and stock market volatility, odds are that the results can be taken seriously. But when one throws the computer at data, looking for just about *any* relationship, it is certain that a spurious connection will emerge, such as the fate of the stock market being linked to the length of women's skirts. And just like the birthday coincidences, it will amaze people.

DATA MINING, STATISTICS, AND CHARLATANISM

What is your probability of winning the New Jersey lottery twice? One in 17 trillion. Yet it happened to Evelyn Adams, whom the reader might guess should feel particularly chosen by destiny. Using the method we developed above, Harvard's Percy Diaconis and Frederick Mosteller estimated at 30 to 1 the probability that someone, somewhere, in a totally unspecified way, gets so lucky!

Some people carry their data mining activities into theology – after all, ancient Mediterraneans used to read potent messages in the entrails of birds. An interesting extension of data mining into biblical exegesis is provided in *The Bible Code* by Michael Drosnin. Drosnin, a former journalist (seemingly innocent of any training in statistics), aided by the works of a "mathematician", helped "predict" Rabin's assassination by deciphering a bible code. He informed Rabin, who obviously did not take it too seriously. *The Bible Code* finds statistical irregularities in the Bible; these help predict some such events. Needless to say that the book sold well.

THE BEST BOOK I HAVE EVER READ!

My favorite time is spent in bookstores, where I aimlessly move from book to book in an attempt to make a decision as to whether to invest the time in reading it. My buying is frequently made on impulse, based on superficial but suggestive clues. Frequently I have nothing but a book jacket as appendage to my decision making. Jackets often contain praise by someone, famous or not, or excerpts from a book review. Good praise by a famous and respected person or a well-known magazine would sway me into buying the book.

What is the problem? I tend to confuse a book review, which is supposed to be an assessment of the quality of the book, with the *best* book reviews, marred with the same survivorship biases. I mistake the distribution of the maximum of a variable with that of the variable itself. The publisher will never put on the jacket of the book anything but the best praise. Some authors go even a step beyond, taking a tepid or even unfavorable book review and selecting words in it that appear to praise the book. One such example came from one Paul Wilmott (an English financial mathematician of rare brilliance and irreverence) who managed to announce that I gave him his "first bad review", yet used excerpts from it as praise on the book jacket (we later became friends, which allowed me to extract an endorsement from him).

The first time I was fooled by this bias was upon buying, when I was 16, *Manhattan Transfer*, a book by John Dos Passos, the American writer, based on praise on the jacket by the philosopher Jean-Paul Sartre, who claimed something to the effect that Dos Passos was the greatest writer of our time. This simple remark, possibly blurted out in a state of intoxication or extreme enthusiasm, caused Dos Passos to become required reading in European intellectual circles, as Sartre's remark was mistaken for a consensus estimate of the quality of Dos Passos rather than what it was, the best remark. (In spite of having received the Nobel Prize in literature, Dos Passos has reverted to obscurity.)

THE BACKTESTER

A programmer helped me build a *backtester*. It is a software program connected to a database of historical prices which allows me to check the hypothetical past performance of any trading rule of average complexity. I can just apply a mechanical trading rule, like buy NASDAQ stocks if they close more than 1.83% above their average of the previous week, and immediately get an idea of its past performance. The screen will flash my hypothetical track record associated with the trading rule. If I do not like the results, I can change the percentage, to say, 1.2%. I can also make the rule more complex. I will keep trying until I find something that works well.

What am I doing? The exact same task of looking for the survivor within the set of rules that can possibly work. I am *fitting* the rule on the data. This activity is called *data snooping*. The more I try, the more I am likely, by mere luck, to find a rule that worked on past data. A random series will always present some detectable pattern. I am convinced that there exists a tradable security in the Western world that would be 100% correlated with the changes in temperature in Oulan Bator, Mongolia.

To get technical, there are even worse extensions. An outstanding recent paper by Sullivan, Timmerman and White[8] goes further and considers that the rules that may be in use successfully today may be the result of a survivorship bias.

Suppose that, over time, investors have experimented with technical trading rules drawn from a very wide universe – in principle thousands of parameterizations of a variety of types of rules. As time progresses, the rules that happen to perform well historically receive more attention and are considered "serious contenders" by the investment community, while unsuccessful trading rules are more likely to be forgotten. ... If enough trading rules are considered over time, some rules are bound by pure luck, even in a very large sample, to produce superior performance even if they do not genuinely possess predictive power over asset returns. Of course, inference based solely on the subset of surviving trading rules may be misleading in this context since it does not account for the full set of initial trading rules, most of which are unlikely to have underperformed.

I have to decry some excesses in back-testing that I have closely witnessed in my private career. There is an excellent product designed just for that, called Omega TradeStation^{TM} that is currently on the market, in use by tens of thousands of traders. It even offers its own computer language. Beset with insomnia, the computerized day-traders become night-testers plowing the data for some of its properties. By dint of throwing their monkeys on typewriters, without specifying what book they want their monkey to write, they will hit upon hypothetical gold somewhere. Many of them blindly believe in it.

One of my colleagues, a man with prestigious degrees, grew to believe in such a virtual world to the point of losing all sense of reality. Whether the modicum of common sense left in him might have rapidly vanished under the mounds of simulations, or whether he might have had none to engage in such pursuit, I cannot tell. By closely watching him I learned that what natural skepticism he may have had vanished under the weight of data – for he was extremely skeptical, but in the wrong area. Ah, Hume!

A MORE UNSETTLING EXTENSION

Historically, medicine has operated by trial and error – in other words, statistically. We know by now that there can be entirely fortuitous connections between symptoms and treatment, and that some medications succeed in medical trials for mere random reasons. I cannot claim expertise in medicine, but have been a steady reader of a segment of the medical literature over the past half decade, long enough to be concerned with the standards, as we will see in the next chapter. Medical researchers are rarely statisticians; statisticians are rarely medical researchers. Many medical researchers are not even remotely aware of this bias. True, it may play a small role, but it is certainly present. One recent medical study links cigarette smoking to a *reduction* in breast cancer, thus conflicting with all previous studies. Logic would indicate that the result may be suspicious, the result of mere coincidence.

THE EARNINGS SEASON: FOOLED BY THE RESULTS

Wall Street analysts, in general, are trained to find the accounting tricks that companies use to hide their earnings. They tend to beat the companies at that game. But they are not trained yet to deal with randomness. When a company shows an increase in earnings once, it draws no immediate attention. Twice, and the name starts showing up on computer screens. Three times, and the company will merit some buy recommendation.

Just as with the track record problem, consider a cohort of 10,000 companies that are assumed on average to barely return the risk-free rate (i.e. Treasury bonds). They engage in all forms of volatile businesses. At the end of the first year, we will have 5,000 "star" companies showing an increase in profits (assuming no inflation), and 5,000 "dogs". After three years, we will have 1,250 "stars". The stock review committee at the investment house will give your broker their name as a "strong buy". He will leave a voice-message that he has a hot recommendation that necessitates immediate action. You will be e-mailed a long list of names. You will buy one or two of them. Meanwhile, the manager in charge of your 401K retirement plan will be acquiring the entire list.

We can apply the reasoning to the selection of investment categories – as if they were the managers in the example above. Assume you are standing in 1900 with hundreds of investments to look at. There are the stock markets of Argentina, Imperial Russia, the United Kingdom, Unified Germany, and plenty of others to consider. A rational person would have bought not just the emerging country of the United States, but those of Russia and Argentina as well. The rest of the story is well known; while many of the stock markets like those of the United Kingdom and the United States fared extremely well, the investor in Imperial Russia would have no better than medium-quality wallpaper in his hands. The countries that fared well are not a large segment of the initial cohort; randomness would be expected to allow a few investment classes to fare extremely well. I wonder if those "experts" who make foolish (and self-serving) statements like "markets will always go up in any 20-year period" are aware of this problem.

CANCER CURES

When I return home from an Asian or European trip, my jet lag often causes me to rise at a very early hour. Occasionally, though very rarely, I switch on the TV set searching for market information. What strikes me in these morning explorations is the abundance of claims by the alternative medicine vendors of the curing power of their products. These no doubt are caused by the lower advertising rates at that time. To prove their claim, they present the convincing testimonial of someone who was cured thanks to their methods. For instance, I once saw a former throat cancer patient explaining how he was saved by a combination of vitamins for sale for the exceptionally low price of $14.95 – in all likelihood he was sincere (although of course compensated for his account, perhaps with a lifetime supply of such medicine). In spite of our advances, people still believe in the existence of links between disease and cure based on such information, and there is no scientific evidence that can convince them more potently than a sincere and emotional testimonial. Such testimonial does not always come from the regular guy; statements by Nobel Prize winners (in the wrong discipline) could easily suffice. Linus Pauling, a Nobel Prize winner in chemistry, was said to believe in vitamin C's medicinal properties, himself ingesting massive daily doses. With his bully pulpit, he contributed to the common belief in vitamin C's curative properties. Many medical studies, unable to replicate Pauling's claims, fell on deaf ears as it was difficult to undo the testimonial by a "Nobel Prize winner", even if he was not qualified to discuss matters related to medicine.

Many of these claims have been harmless outside of the financial profits for these charlatans – but many cancer patients may have replaced the more scientifically investigated therapies, in favor of these methods and died as a result of their neglecting more orthodox cures (again, the nonscientific methods are gathered under what is called "alternative medicine", that is, unproven therapies and the medical community has difficulties convincing the press that there is only one medicine and that alternative medicine is not medicine). The reader might wonder about my claims that the user of these products could be sincere, without it meaning that he was cured by the illusory treatment. The reason is something called "spontaneous remission", in which a very small minority of cancer patients, for reasons that remain entirely speculative, wipe out cancer cells and recover "miraculously". Some switch causes the patient's immune system to eradicate all cancer cells from the body. These people would have been equally cured by drinking a glass of Vermont spring water or chewing on dried beef as they were by taking these beautifully wrapped pills. Finally, these spontaneous remissions might not be so spontaneous; they might, at the bottom, have a cause that we are not yet sophisticated enough to detect.

The late astronomer Carl Sagan, a devoted promoter of scientific thinking and an obsessive enemy of non-science, examined the cures from cancer that result from a visit to Lourdes in France where people were healed by simple contact with the holy waters, and found out the interesting fact that, of the total cancer patients who visited the place, the cure rate was, if anything, lower than the statistical one for spontaneous remissions. It was lower than the average for those who did not go to Lourdes! Should a statistician infer here that cancer patients' odds of surviving deteriorates after a visit to Lourdes?

PROFESSOR PEARSON GOES TO MONTE CARLO (LITERALLY): RANDOMNESS DOES NOT LOOK RANDOM!

At the beginning of the twentieth century, as we were starting to develop techniques to deal with the notion of random outcomes, several methods were designed to detect anomalies. Professor Karl Pearson (of Neyman-Pearson fame, familiar to every person who sat in a statistics 101 class) devised the first test of non-randomness (it was in reality a test of deviation from normality, which, for all intents and purposes, was the same thing). He examined millions of runs of what was called a Monte Carlo (the old name for a roulette wheel) during the month of July 1902. He discovered that, with a high degree of statistical significance (with an error of less than one to a billion), the runs were not purely random. What! The roulette wheel was not random! Professor Pearson was greatly surprised at the discovery. But this result in itself tells us nothing; we know that there is no such thing as a pure random draw, for the outcome of the draw depends on the quality of the equipment. With enough minutiae one would be able to uncover the non-randomness somewhere (i.e. the wheel itself may not have been perfectly balanced or perhaps the spinning ball was not completely spherical). Philosophers of statistics call this the *reference case problem*, to explain that there is no true attainable randomness in practice, only in theory. Besides, a manager would question whether such non-randomness can lead to any meaningful profitable rules. If I need to gamble $1 on 10,000 runs and expect to make $1 for my efforts, then I would do much better in the part-time employment of a janitorial agency.

But the result bears another suspicious element. Of more practical relevance here is the following severe problem about non-randomness. Even the fathers of statistical science forgot that a random series of runs need not exhibit a pattern to look random; as a matter of fact data that is perfectly patternless would be extremely suspicious and appear to be man-made. A single random run is bound to exhibit some pattern – if one looks hard enough. Note that Professor Pearson was among the first scholars who were interested in creating artificial random data generators, tables one could use as inputs for various scientific and engineering simulations (the precursors of our Monte Carlo simulator). The problem is that they did not want these tables to exhibit any form of regularity. Yet real randomness does not look random!

I would further illustrate the point with the study of a phenomenon well known as cancer clusters. Consider a square with 16 random darts hitting it with equal probability of being at any place in the square. If we divide the square into 16 smaller squares, it is expected that each smaller square will contain one dart on average – but only on average. There is a very small probability of having exactly 16 darts in 16 different squares. The average grid will have more than one dart in a few squares, and no dart at all in many squares. It will be an exceptionally rare incident that no (cancer) cluster would show on the grid. Now, transpose our grid with the darts in it to overlay a map of any region. Some newspaper will declare that one of the areas (the one with more than the average of darts) harbors radiation that causes cancer, prompting lawyers to start soliciting the patients.

THE DOG THAT DID NOT BARK: ON BIASES IN SCIENTIFIC KNOWLEDGE

By the same argument, science is marred by a pernicious survivorship bias, affecting the way research gets published. In a way that is similar to journalism, research that yields no result does not make it to print.

That may seem sensible, as newspapers do not have to have a screaming headline saying that nothing new is taking place (though the Bible was smart enough to declare *ein chadash tacht hashemesh* – "nothing new under the sun", providing the information that things just do recur). The problem is that a finding of absence and an absence of findings get mixed together. There may be great information in the fact that *nothing took place*. As Sherlock Holmes noted in the *Silver Blaze* case – the curious thing was that the dog did not bark. More problematically, there are plenty of scientific results that are left out of publications because they are not statistically significant, but nevertheless provide information.[9]

I Have No Conclusion

I am frequently asked the question: when is it truly not luck? To be honest, I am unable to answer it. I can tell that person A seems less lucky than person B, but the confidence in such knowledge can be so weak as to be meaningless. I prefer to remain a skeptic. People frequently misinterpret my opinion. I never said that every rich man is an idiot and every unsuccessful person unlucky, only that in absence of much additional information I prefer to reserve my judgment. It is safer.

✛

TEN

LOSER TAKES ALL - ON THE NONLINEARITIES OF LIFE

The nonlinear viciousness of life. Moving to Bel Air and acquiring the vices of the rich and famous. Why Microsoft's Bill Gates may not be the best in his business (but please do not inform him of such a fact). Depriving donkeys of food.

Next I put the platitude that *life is unfair* under some examination, but in a new angle. The twist: life is unfair in a *nonlinear* way. This chapter is about how a small advantage in life can translate into a highly disproportionate payoff, or, more viciously, how no advantage at all, but a very, very small help from randomness, can lead to a bonanza.

The Sandpile Effect

First we define nonlinearity. There are many ways to present it, but one of the most popular ones in science is what is called the sandpile effect, which I can illustrate as follows. I am currently sitting on a beach in

Copacabana, in Rio de Janeiro, attempting to do nothing strenuous, away from anything to read and write (unsuccessfully, of course, as I am mentally writing these lines). I am playing with plastic beach toys borrowed from a child, trying to build an edifice – modestly but doggedly attempting to emulate the tower of Babel. I continuously add sand to the top, slowly raising the entire structure. My Babylonian relatives thought they could thus reach the heavens. I have more humble designs; to test how high I could go before it would topple. I keep adding sand, testing to see how the structure would ultimately collapse. Unused to seeing adults build sandcastles, a child looks at me with amazement.

In time – and much to the onlooking child's delight – my castle inevitably topples to rejoin the rest of the sand on the beach. It could be said that the last grain of sand is responsible for the destruction of the entire structure. What we are witnessing here is a nonlinear effect resulting from a linear force exerted on an object. A very small additional input, here the grain of sand, caused a disproportionate result, namely the destruction of my starter tower of Babel. Popular wisdom has integrated many such phenomena, as witnessed by such expressions as "the straw that broke the camel's back" or "the drop that caused the water to spill".

These nonlinear dynamics have a bookstore name; chaos theory, which is a misnomer because it has nothing to do with chaos. Chaos theory concerns itself primarily with functions in which a small input can lead to a disproportionate response. Population models, for instance, can lead to a path of explosive growth, or extinction of a species, depending on a very small difference in the population at a starting point in time. Another popular scientific analogy is the weather, where it has been shown that a simple butterfly fluttering its wings in India can cause a hurricane in New York. But the classics have their share to offer as well: Pascal (the same of Pascal's wager in Chapter 7) said that if Cleopatra's nose had been slightly shorter, the world's fate would have changed. Cleopatra had comely features dominated by a thin and elongated nose that made Julius Caesar and his successor Marc Antony fall for her (here the intellectual snob in me cannot resist dissenting against conventional wisdom; Plutarch claimed that it was Cleopatra's skills in conversation, rather than her good looks, that caused the maddening infatuation of the shakers and movers of her day; I truly believe it).

ENTER RANDOMNESS

Things can become more interesting when randomness enters the game. Imagine a waiting room full of actors queuing for an audition. The number of actors who will win is clearly small, and they are the ones generally observed by the public as representative of the profession, as we saw in our discussion on survivorship bias. The winners would move into Bel Air, feel pressure to acquire some basic training in the consumption of luxury goods and, perhaps owing to the dissolute and unrhythmic lifestyle, flirt with substance abuse. As to the others (the great majority), we can imagine their fate; a lifetime of serving foamed *caffe latte* at the neighboring Starbucks, fighting the biological clock between auditions.

One may argue that the actor who lands the lead role that catapulted him into fame and expensive swimming pools has some skills others lack, some charm, or a specific physical trait that was a perfect match for such a career path. I beg to differ. The winner may have had some acting skills, but so do all of the others, otherwise they would not have been in the waiting room.

It is an interesting attribute of fame that it has its own dynamics. An actor becomes known by some parts of the public because he is known by other parts of the public. The dynamics of such fame follow a rotating helix, which may have started at the audition, as the selection could have been caused by some silly detail that fitted the mood of the examiner on that day. Had the examiner not fallen in love the previous day with a person of similar sounding last name, then our selected actor from that particular sample *history* would be serving *caffe latte* in the intervening sample *history*.

LEARNING TO TYPE

Researchers frequently use the example of QWERTY to describe the vicious dynamics of winning and losing in an economy, and to illustrate how the final outcome is more than frequently the undeserved one. The arrangement of the letters on a typewriter is an example of the success of the least deserving method. For our typewriters have the orders of the letters on their keyboard arranged in a non-optimal manner, as a matter of fact in such a non-optimal manner as to slow down the typing rather than make the job easy, in order to avoid jamming the ribbons as they were designed for less electronic days. Therefore, as we started building better typewriters and computerized word processors, several attempts were made to rationalize the computer keyboard, to no avail. People were trained on a QWERTY keyboard and their habits were too sticky for change. Just like the helical propulsion of an actor into stardom, people patronize what other people like to do. Forcing a rational dynamic on the process would be superfluous, nay, impossible. This is called a *path dependent outcome*, and has thwarted many mathematical attempts at modeling behavior.

It is obvious that the information age, by homogenizing our tastes, is causing the unfairness to be even more acute – those who win capture almost all the customers. The example that strikes most as the most spectacular lucky success is that of the software maker Microsoft and its moody founder Bill Gates. While it is hard to deny that Gates is a man of high personal standards, work ethics, and above average intelligence, is he the best? Does he *deserve* it? Clearly not. Most people are equipped with his software (like myself) because other people are equipped with his software, a purely circular effect (economists call that "network externalities"). Nobody ever claimed that it was the best software product. Most of Gates's rivals have an obsessive jealousy of his success. There are maddened by the fact that he managed to win so big while many of them are struggling to make their companies survive.

Such ideas go against classical economic models, in which results either come from a precise reason (there is no account for uncertainty) or the good guy wins (the good guy is the one who is more skilled and has some technical superiority). Economists discovered path-dependent effects late in their game, then tried to publish wholesale on the topic that otherwise would be bland and obvious. For instance, Brian Arthur, an economist concerned with nonlinearities at the Santa Fe Institute, wrote that chance events coupled with positive feedback rather than technological superiority will determine economic superiority – not some abstrusely defined edge in a given area of expertise. While early economic models excluded randomness, Arthur explained how "unexpected orders, chance meetings with lawyers, managerial whims

... would help determine which ones achieved early sales and, over time, which firms dominated".

Mathematics Inside and Outside the Real World

A mathematical approach to the problem is in order. While in conventional models (such as the well-known Brownian random walk used in finance) the probability of success does not change with every incremental step, only the accumulated wealth, Arthur suggests models such as the Polya process, which is mathematically very difficult to work with, but can be easily understood with the aid of a Monte Carlo simulator. The Polya process can be presented as follows: assume an urn initially containing equal quantities of black and red balls. You are to guess each time which color you will pull out before you make the draw. Here the game is rigged. Unlike a conventional urn, the probability of guessing correctly depends on past success, as you get better or worse at guessing depending on past performance. Thus the probability of winning increases after past wins, that of losing increases after past losses. Simulating such a process, one can see a huge variance of outcomes, with astonishing successes and large number of failures (what we called skewness).

Compare such a process with those that are more commonly modeled, that is, an urn from which the player makes guesses with replacement. Say you played roulette and won. Would this increase your chances of winning again? No. In a Polya process case, it does. Why is this so mathematically hard to work with? Because the notion of independence (i.e., when the next draw does not depend on past outcomes) is violated. Independence is a requirement for working with the (known) math of probability.

What has gone wrong with the development of economics as a science? Answer: there was a bunch of intelligent people who felt compelled to use mathematics just to tell themselves that they were rigorous in their thinking, that theirs was a science. Someone in a great rush decided to introduce mathematical modeling techniques (culprits:

Leon Walras, Gerard Debreu, Paul Samuelson) without considering the fact that either the class of mathematics they were using was too restrictive for the class of problems they were dealing with, or that perhaps they should be aware that the precision of the language of mathematics could lead people to believe that they had solutions when in fact they had none (recall Popper and the costs of taking science too seriously). Indeed the mathematics they dealt with did not work in the real world, possibly because we needed richer classes of processes – and they refused to accept the fact that no mathematics at all was probably better.

The so-called *complexity theorists* came to the rescue. Much excitement was generated by the works of scientists who specialized in nonlinear quantitative methods – the Mecca of those being the Santa Fe Institute near Santa Fe, New Mexico. Clearly these scientists are trying hard, and providing us with wonderful solutions in the physical sciences and better models in the social siblings (though nothing satisfactory there yet). And if they ultimately do not succeed, it will simply be because mathematics may be of only secondary help in our real world. Note another advantage of Monte Carlo simulations is that we can get results where mathematics fails us and can be of no help. In freeing us from equations it frees us from the traps of inferior mathematics. As I said in Chapter 4, mathematics is merely a way of thinking and meditating, little more, in our world of randomness.

BURIDAN'S DONKEY OR THE GOOD SIDE OF RANDOMNESS

Nonlinearity in random outcomes is sometimes used as a tool to break stalemates. Consider the problem of the nonlinear nudge. Imagine a donkey equally hungry and thirsty placed at exactly equal distance from two sources of food and water. In such a framework, he would die of both thirst and hunger as he would be unable to decide which one to get to first. Now inject some randomness in the picture, by randomly nudging the donkey, causing him to get closer to one source, no matter which, and accordingly away from the other. The impasse would be instantly broken and our happy donkey will be either in turn well fed then well hydrated, or well hydrated then well fed.

The reader no doubt has played a version of Buridan's donkey, by "flipping a coin" to break some of the minor stalemates in life where one lets randomness help with the decision process. Let Lady Fortuna make the decision and gladly submit. I often use Buridan's donkey (under its mathematical name) when my computer goes into a freeze between two alternatives (to be technical, these "randomizations" are frequently done during optimization problems, when one needs to perturbate a function).

Note that Buridan's donkey was named after the fourteenth-century philosopher Jean Buridan. Buridan had an interesting death (he was thrown in the Seine tied in a bag and died drowning). This tale was considered an example of sophistry by his contemporaries who missed the import of randomization – Buridan was clearly ahead of his time.

When It Rains, It Pours

As I am writing these lines, I am opening my fund to investors and exploring how to raise money. I am suddenly realizing that the world's bi-polarity is hitting me very hard. Either one succeeds wildly, by attracting all the cash, or fails to draw a single penny. Likewise with books. Either everyone wants to publish it, or nobody is interested in returning telephone calls (in the latter case my discipline is to delete the name from my address book). This is making me, with my profound and antiquated Mediterranean sense of *metrion* (measure) extremely uncomfortable, even queasy. Too much success is the enemy (think of the punishment meted out on the rich and famous), too much failure is demoralizing. I would like the option of having neither.

ELEVEN

RANDOMNESS AND OUR BRAIN: WE ARE PROBABILITY BLIND

On the difficulty of thinking of your vacation as a linear combination of Paris and the Bahamas. Nero Tulip may never ski in the Alps again. Some discussion of behavioral discoveries. Some manifestations of probability blindness taken out of a textbook. A little more on journalistic pollution. Why you may be dead by now.

Paris or the Bahamas?

You have two options for your next brief vacation in March. The first is to fly to Paris; the second is to go to the Caribbean. You expressed indifference between the two options; your spouse will tip the decision one way or the other. Two distinct and separate images come to you when you think of the possibilities. In the first one, you see yourself standing at the Musée d'Orsay in front of some Pissaro painting depicting a cloudy sky – the gray Parisian wintry sky. You are carrying an umbrella under your arm. In the second image, you are lying on a towel with a stack of books by your favorite authors next to you (Tom Clancy and Amianus Marcellinus), and an obsequious waiter serving you a banana daiquiri. You know that the two states are mutually exclusive (you can only be in one place at one time), but exhaustive (there is a 100% probability that you will be in one of them). They are equiprobable, with, in your opinion, 50% probability assigned to each.

You derive great pleasure thinking about your vacation; it motivates you and makes your daily commute more bearable. But the adequate way to visualize yourself, according to rational behavior under uncertainty, is 50% in one of the vacation spots and 50% in the other – what is mathematically called a *linear combination* of the two states. Can your brain handle that? How desirable would it be to have your feet in the Caribbean waters and your head exposed to the Parisian rain? Our brain can properly handle one and only one state at once – unless you have personality troubles of a deeply pathological nature. Now try to imagine an 85%/15% combination. Any luck?

Consider a bet you make with a colleague for the amount of $1,000, which, in your opinion, is exactly fair. Tomorrow night you will have zero or $2,000 in your pocket, each with a 50% probability. In purely mathematical terms, the fair value of a bet is the linear combination of the states, here called the *mathematical expectation*, i.e., the probabilities of each payoff multiplied by the dollar values at stake (50% multiplied by 0 and 50% multiplied by $2,000 = $1,000). Can you *imagine* (that is visualize, not compute mathematically) the value being $1,000? We can conjure up one and only *one* state at a given time. Left to our own devices, we are likely to bet in an irrational way, as one of the states would dominate the picture.

Some Architectural Considerations

Time to reveal Nero's secret. It was a black swan. He was then 35. Although pre-war buildings in New York can have a pleasant front, their architecture seen from the back offers a stark contrast by being completely bland. The doctor's examination room had a window overlooking the backyard of one such Upper East side street, and Nero will always remember how bland that backyard was in comparison with the front, even if he were to live another half century. He will always remember the view of the ugly pink backyard from the leaden window panes, and the medical diploma on the wall that he read a dozen times as he was waiting for the doctor to come into the room (half an eternity, for Nero suspected that something was wrong). The news was then delivered (grave voice), "I have some ... I got the pathology report ... It's ... It is not as bad as it sounds ... It's ... It's cancer". The declaration caused his body to be hit by an electric discharge, running through his back down to his knees. Nero tried to yell "what?" but no sound came out of his mouth. What scared him was not so much the news as the sight of the doctor. Somehow the news reached his body before his mind. There was too much fear in the doctor's eyes and Nero immediately suspected that the news was even worse than what he was being told (it was).

The night of the diagnosis, at the medical library where he sat, drenched wet from walking for hours in the rain without noticing it and making a puddle of water around him (he was yelled at by an attendant but could not concentrate on what she was saying so she shrugged her shoulders and walked away); later he read the sentence "72% 5-year actuarially adjusted survival rate". It meant that 72 people out of a hundred make it. It takes between three and five years for the body without clinical manifestations of the disease for the patient to be pronounced cured (closer to three at his age). He then felt in his guts quite certain that he was going to make it.

Now the reader might wonder about the mathematical difference between a 28% chance of death and a 72% chance of survival over the next five years. Clearly, there is none, but we are not made for mathematics. In Nero' mind a 28% chance of death meant the image of himself dead, and thoughts of the cumbersome details of his funeral. A 72% chance of survival put him in a cheerful mood; his mind was planning the result of a cured Nero skiing in the Alps. At no point during his ordeal did Nero think of himself as 72% alive and 28% dead.

From Psychology to Neurobiology

For reasons we just saw, the laws of probability are said to be counterintuitive by the researchers in the cognitive and behavioral sciences. We are *probability blind*, these scientists say. This chapter will rapidly illustrate some manifestations of such blindness, with a cursory exposition of the research in that area.

The idea of probability blindness gave rise to an entire discipline dedicated to the study of the effect these biases carry on our behavior. It is filling out library shelves and causing the creation of numerous investment funds dedicated to the sister idea that people do not behave in a rational way in the markets. Some funds have been built around the idea that people overreact to news, while others have been devoted to the notion that, to the contrary, people underreact (I was told early in my career that the more diversity the better for the market). These beliefs give rise to two categories of trading strategies. On one side we find the contrarians who subscribe to the following rationale: *Hey, since people systematically overreact, let us take the other side, sell the winners and buy the losers.* On the other side stand the momentum players who do the exact opposite: *Since markets do not adjust fast enough, let us buy the winners and sell the losers.* Because of randomness, both categories will show periodic victories, which cannot prove directly that either theory is right or wrong.

Even psychiatrists and clinical psychologists are joining the fray by becoming "experts" – after all they know more about the human mind that those financial economists with their unrealistic, unscientific equations, and it is, after all, human behavior that ultimately influences the markets. A yearly conference in Boston gathers medical doctors and psychology researchers musing over market strategies. The idea may seem simple, perhaps even boring until we encounter professionals, whom we expect would deal with the matter with maximal expertise, falling right into the trap like the man on the street.

OUR NATURAL HABITAT

I will not delve too deeply into amateur evolutionary theory to probe at the reasons (besides, in spite of having spent some time in libraries I feel that I am truly an amateur in the subject matter). Clearly, the environment for which we have built our genetic endowment is not the one that prevails today. I have not told too many of my colleagues that their decision-making contains some lingering habits of cavemen – but when markets experience an abrupt move, I experience the same rush of adrenaline as if a leopard was seen prowling near my trading desk. Some of my colleagues who break telephone handles upon losing money might be even closer in their psychological makeup to our common origin.

This might be a platitude to those who frequent the Greek and Latin classics, but we never fail to be surprised when noticing that people a couple of dozen centuries removed from us can exhibit similar sensibility and feelings. What used to strike me as a child upon visiting museums is that ancient Greek statues exhibit men with traits indistinguishable from ours (only more harmonious and aristocratic). I was so wrong to believe that 2,200 years was a long time. Proust wrote frequently about the surprise people have while coming across emotions in Homeric heroes that are similar to those we experience today. By genetic standards, these Homeric heroes of 30 centuries ago in all likelihood have the exact identical genetic makeup as the pudgy middle-aged man you see schlepping groceries in the parking lot. More than that. In fact we are truly identical to the man who perhaps 80 centuries ago started being called "civilized", in that strip of land stretching from Southeastern Syria to Southwestern Mesopotamia.

What is our natural habitat? By natural habitat, I mean the environment in which we reproduced the most, the one in which we spent the highest number of generations. The consensus among anthropologists is that we have been around as a separate species for 130,000 years, most of which were spent in the African savannah. But we do not have to go back that far in history to get the point. Imagine life in an early urban settlement, in Middle-Town, Fertile Crescent, only about 3,000 years ago – surely modern times from a genetic standpoint. Information is limited by the physical means of its transmission; one cannot travel fast, hence information will come from faraway places in concise batches. Traveling is a nuisance fraught with all manner of physical danger; you will settle within a narrow radius of where you were born unless famine or some invading uncivilized tribe dislodges you and your relatives from your happy settlement. The number of people you would get to know in a lifetime will be small. Should a crime be committed, it will be easy to gauge the evidence of guilt within the small number of possible suspects. If you are unjustly convicted of a crime, you will argue in simple terms, propounding simple evidence like "I was not there as I was praying in the temple of Baal and was seen at dusk by the high priest" and add that Obedshemesh son of Sahar was more likely to be guilty because he had more to gain from the crime. Your life would be simple, hence your space of *probabilities* would be narrow.

The real problem is, as I have mentioned, that such a natural habitat does not include much information. An efficient computation of the odds was never necessary until very recently. This explains why we had to wait until the emergence of the gambling literature to see the growth of the mathematics of probability. Popular belief holds that the religious backdrop of the first and second millennium blocked the growth of tools that hint at absence of determinism, and caused the delays in probability research. The idea is extremely dubious; we simply did not compute probabilities because we did not *dare* to? Surely the reason is rather because we did not *need* to. Much of our problem comes from the fact that we have evolved out of such a habitat faster, much faster than our genes. Even worse; our genes have not changed at all.

KAFKA IN A COURTROOM

The O.J. Simpson trial provides an example of how our modern society is ruled by probability (because of the explosion in information), while important decisions are made without the smallest regard for its basic laws. We are capable of sending a spacecraft to Mars, but we are incapable of having criminal trials managed by the basic laws of probability – yet evidence is clearly a probabilistic notion. I remember buying a book on probability at a Borders Books chain bookstore only a short distance from the Los Angeles courthouse where the "trial of the century" was taking place – another book that crystallized the highly sophisticated quantitative knowledge in the field. How could such a leap in knowledge elude lawyers and jurors only a few miles away?

People who are as close to being criminal as probability laws can allow us to infer (that is with a confidence that exceeds the *shadow of a doubt*) are walking free because of our misunderstanding of basic concepts of the odds. You could be convicted for a crime you never committed owing to a poor reading of probability – for we still cannot have a court of law properly compute the joint probability of events (the probability of two events taking place at the same time). I was in a dealing room with a TV set turned on when I saw one of the lawyers arguing that there were at least four people in Los Angeles capable of carrying O.J. Simpson's DNA characteristics (thus ignoring the joint set of events – we will see how in the next paragraph). I then switched off the television set in disgust, causing an uproar among the traders. I was under the impression until then that sophistry had been eliminated from legal cases thanks to the high standards of republican Rome. Worse, one Harvard lawyer used the specious argument that only 10% of men who brutalize their wives go on to murder them, which is a probability unconditional on the murder (whether the statement was made out of a warped notion of advocacy, pure malice, or ignorance is immaterial). Isn't the law devoted to the truth? The correct way to look at it is to determine the percentage of murder cases where women were killed by their husband *and* had previously been battered by him (that is, 50%) – for we are dealing with what is called *conditional* probabilities; the probability that O.J. killed his wife *conditional* on the information of her having been killed, rather than the *unconditional* probability of O.J. killing his wife. How can we expect the untrained person to understand randomness when a Harvard professor who deals and teaches the concept of probabilistic evidence can make such an incorrect statement?

More particularly, where jurors (and lawyers) tend to make mistakes, along with the rest of us, is in the notion of joint probability. They do not realize that evidence compounds. The probability of my being diagnosed with respiratory tract cancer and being run over by a pink Cadillac in the same year, assuming each one of them is 1/100,000, becomes 1/10,000,000,000 – by multiplying the two (obviously independent) events. Arguing that O.J. Simpson had 1/500,000 chance of not being the killer from the blood standpoint (the lawyers used the sophistry that there were four people with such blood types walking around Los Angeles) and adding to it the fact that he was the husband of the person and that there was additional evidence, then (owing to the compounding effect) the odds against him rise to several trillion trillion.

"Sophisticated" people make worse mistakes. I can surprise people by saying that the probability of the joint event is lower than either. Behavioral economists submitted rational and educated people (graduate students) to tests where they needed to produce the probability of a young woman with a liberal arts education being a *bank teller* or a *feminist bank teller*. They assigned on average a higher probability to her being a feminist bank teller than to that of her being a bank teller. I am glad to be a trader taking advantage of people's biases but I am scared of living in such a society.

AN ABSURD WORLD

Kafka's prophetic book, *The Trial*, about the plight of a man, Joseph K., who is arrested for a mysterious and unexplained reason hit a spot as it was written before we heard of the methods of the "scientific" totalitarian regimes. It projected a scary future of mankind wrapped in absurd self-feeding bureaucracies, with spontaneously emerging rules subjected to the internal logic of the bureaucracy. It spawned an entire literature of the *absurd*; the world may be too incongruous for us. I am terrified of certain lawyers. After listening to statements during the O.J. trial (and their effect) I was scared, truly scared of the possible outcome; my being arrested for some reason that made no sense probabilistically, and having to fight some glib lawyer in front of a randomness illiterate jury.

We said that mere judgment would probably suffice in a primitive society. It is easy for a society to live without mathematics – or traders to trade without quantitative methods – when the space of possible outcomes is one dimensional. One dimensional means that we are looking at one sole variable, not a collection of separate events. The price of one security is one dimensional, whereas the collection of the prices of several securities is multidimensional and requires mathematical modeling – we cannot easily see the collection of possible outcomes of the portfolio with a naked eye, and cannot even represent it on a graph as our physical world has been limited to visual representation in three dimensions only. We will argue later why we run the risk of having bad models (admittedly, we have) or making the error of condoning ignorance – swinging between the Carybde of the lawyer who knows no math to the Scylla of the mathematician who misuses his math because he does not have the judgment to select the right model. In other words, we will have to swing between the mistake of listening to the glib nonsense of a lawyer who refuses science and that of applying the flawed theories of some economist who takes his science too seriously. The beauty of science is that it makes an allowance for both error types. Luckily, there is a middle road – but sadly, it is rarely traveled.

KAHNEMAN AND TVERSKY

Who are the most influential economists of the century, in terms of journal references, their followings, and their influence over the profession? No, it is not John Maynard Keynes, not Alfred Marshall, not Paul Samuelson, and certainly not Milton Friedman. They are Daniel Kahneman and Amos Tversky, psychology researchers whose specialty was to uncover areas where human beings are not endowed with rational thinking and optimal economic behavior.

The pair taught us a lot about the way we perceive and handle uncertainty. Their research, conducted on a population of students and professors in the early 1970s, showed that we do not correctly understand contingencies. Furthermore, they showed that in the rare cases when we understand probability, we do not seem to consider it in our behavior. Since the Kahneman and Tversky results, an entire discipline called *behavioral finance and economics* has flourished. It is in open contradiction with the orthodox so-called *neoclassical economics* taught in business schools under the normative names of *efficient markets*, *rational expectations*, and other such concepts. It is worth stopping, at this juncture, and discussing the distinction between normative and positive sciences. A *normative* science (clearly a self-contradictory concept) offers prescriptive teachings; it studies how things *should* be. Some economists, for example, (those of the efficient market religion) believe that humans are rational and act rationally because it is the best thing for them to do (it is mathematically "optimal"). The opposite is a *positive* science, which is based on how people actually are observed to behave. In spite of economists' envy of physicists, physics is an inherently positive science while economics, particularly microeconomics and financial economics, is predominantly a normative one.

NEUROBIOLOGY

The soft sciences of psychology and economics have cheated us on occasions in the past. How? Economics has produced laughable ideas, ideas that evaporate once one changes the assumptions a little bit. It seems difficult to take sides with bickering economists trading often-incomprehensible arguments (even to economists). Biology and medicine, on the other hand, rank higher in scientific firmness; like *true* sciences, they can explain things while at the same time being subjected to falsification. They are both positive and their theories are *better* theories, that is, more easily testable. The good news is that neurologists are starting to confirm these results, with what is called environment mapping in the brain, by taking a patient whose brain is damaged in one single spot (say, by a tumor or an injury deemed to be local) and deducing by elimination the function performed by such part of the anatomy. This isolates the parts of the brain that perform the various functions. The Kahneman and Tversky results thus found a *terra firma* with the leaps in our knowledge obtained through behavioral genetics and, further, plain medicine. Some of the physiology of our brain makes us perceive things and behave in a given manner. We are, whether we like it or not, prisoners of our biology.

Researchers in evolutionary psychology provide convincing reasons for these biases. We have not had the incentive to develop an ability to understand probability because we did not have to do so – but the more profound reason is that we are not designed to understand things. We are built only to survive and procreate. To survive, we need to overstate some probabilities, such as those that can affect our survival. For instance, those whose brain imparted higher odds to dangers of death, in other words the paranoid, survived and gave us their genes (provided such paranoia did not come at too high a cost, otherwise it would have been a drawback). Our brain has been wired with biases that may hamper us in a more complex environment, one that requires a more accurate assessment of probabilities.

The story of these biases is thus being corroborated by the various disciplines; the magnitude of the perceptional distortions makes us less than rational, in the sense of both having coherent beliefs (i.e. free of logical contradictions) and acting in a manner compatible with these beliefs.

EXAMPLES OF BIASES IN UNDERSTANDING PROBABILITY

I found in the behavioral literature at least 40 damning examples of such acute biases. Below is the account of a well-known test, and an embarrassing one for the medical profession. The following quiz was given to medical doctors (which I borrowed from the excellent Deborah Bennett's *Randomness*).

> *A test of a disease presents a rate of 5% false positives. The disease strikes 1/1,000 of the population. People are tested at random, regardless of whether they are suspected of having the disease. A patient's test is positive. What is the probability of the patient being stricken with the disease?*[10]

Most doctors answered 95%, simply taking into account the fact that the test has a 95% accuracy rate. The answer is the conditional probability that the patient is sick and the test shows it – close to 2%. Less than one in five professionals got it right.

I will simplify the answer. Assume no false negatives. Consider that out of 1,000 patients who are administered the test, one will be expected to be afflicted with the disease. Out of a population of the remaining 999 healthy patients, the test will identify about 50 with the disease (it is 95% accurate). The correct answer should be that the probability of being afflicted with the disease for someone selected at random who presented a positive test is the following ratio:

$$\frac{\text{Number of afflicted persons}}{\text{Number of true and false positives}}$$

here 1 in 51.

Think of the number of times you will be given a medication that carries damaging side effects for a given disease you were told you had, when you may only have 2% probability of being afflicted with it!

WE ARE OPTION BLIND

As an option trader, I have noticed that people tend to undervalue options as they are usually unable to correctly mentally evaluate instruments that deliver an *uncertain* payoff, even when they are fully conscious of the mathematics. Even regulators reinforce such ignorance by explaining to people that options are a *decaying* or *wasting* asset. Options that are out of the money are deemed to *decay*, by losing their premium between two dates.

I will clarify next with a simplified (but sufficient) explanation of what an option means. Say a stock trades at $100 and that someone gives me the right (but not the obligation) to buy it at $110 one month ahead of today. This is dubbed a *call* option. It only makes sense for me to *exercise* it, by asking the seller of the option to deliver me the stock at $110, if it trades at a higher price than $110 in one month's time. If the stock goes to $120, my option will be worth $10, for I will be able to buy the stock at $110 from the option writer and sell it to the market at $120, pocketing the difference. But this does not have a very high probability. It is called *out-of-the-money*, for I have no gain from exercising it right away.

Consider that I buy the option for $1. What do I expect the value of the option to be one month from now? Most people think 0. That is not true. The option has a high probability, say 90% of being worth 0 at expiration, but perhaps 10% probability to be worth an average of $10. Thus, selling the option to me for $1 does not provide the seller with free money. If the sellers had instead bought the stock themselves at $100 and waited the month, they could have sold it for $120. Making $1 now was hardly, therefore, free money. Likewise, buying it is not a wasting asset. Even professionals can be fooled. How? They confuse the expected value and the most likely scenario (here the expected value is $1 and the most likely scenario is for the option to be worth 0). They mentally overweigh the state that is the most likely, namely, that the market does not move at all. The option is simply the weighted average of the possible states the asset can take.

There is another type of satisfaction provided by the option seller. It is the steady return and the steady feeling of reward – what psychologists call *flow*. It is very pleasant to go to work in the morning with the expectation of being up some small money. It requires some strength of character to accept the expectation of bleeding a little, losing pennies on a steady basis even if the strategy is bound to be profitable over longer periods. I noticed that very few option traders can maintain what I call a "long volatility" position, namely a position that will most likely lose a small quantity of money at expiration, but is expected to make money in the long run because of occasional spurts. I discovered very few people who accepted losing $1 for most expirations and making $10 once in a while, even if the game were fair (i.e., they made the $10 more than 10% of the time).

I divide the community of option traders into two categories: *premium sellers* and *premium buyers*. Premium sellers (also called option sellers) sell options, and generally make steady money, like John in Chapters 1 and 5. Premium buyers do the reverse. Option sellers, it is said, eat like chickens and go to the bathroom like elephants. Alas, most option traders I encountered in my career are *premium sellers* – when they blow up it is generally other people's money.

How could professionals seemingly aware of the (simple) mathematics be put in such a position? Our understanding of math can remain quite superficial; medicine is starting to believe that our actions are not quite guided by the parts of our brain that dictate rationality (see Antonio Damasio's *Descartes' Error* or Ledoux's *Emotional Brain*[11]). We think with our emotions and there is no way around it. For the same reason, people who are otherwise rational engage in smoking or in fights that get them no immediate benefits, likewise people sell options even when they know that it is not a good thing to do. But things can get worse. There is a category of people, generally academics, who, instead of fitting their actions to their brains, instead fit their brains to their actions. These go back and cheat with the statistics to justify their actions. In my business, they fool themselves with statistical arguments to justify their option selling.

Probabilities and the Media (More Journalists)

A journalist is trained in methods to express himself rather than to plumb the depth of things – the selection process favors the most communicative, not necessarily the most knowledgeable. My medical doctor friends claim that many medical journalists do not understand anything about medicine and biology, often making mistakes of a very basic nature. I cannot confirm such statements, being myself a mere amateur (though at times a voracious reader) in medical research but I have noticed that they almost always misunderstand the probabilities used in medical research announcements. The most common one concerns the interpretation of evidence. They most commonly get mixed up between *absence of evidence* and *evidence of absence*, a similar problem to the one we saw in Chapter 9. How? Say I test some chemotherapy, say Fluorouracil for upper respiratory tract cancer, and find that it is better than a placebo, but only marginally so; that (in addition to other modalities) it improves survival from 21 per 100 to 24 per 100. Given my sample size, I may not be confident that the additional 3% survival points come from the medicine; it could be merely attributable to randomness. I would write a paper outlining my results and saying that there is no evidence of improved survival (as yet) from such medicine, and that further research would be needed. A medical journalist would pick it up and claim that one Professor N.N. Taleb found evidence that Fluorouracil *does not help*, which is entirely opposite to my intentions. Some naïve doctor in Smalltown, even more uncomfortable with probabilities than the most untrained journalist, would pick it up and build a mental block against the medication, even when some researcher finally finds fresh evidence that such medicine confers a clear survival advantage.

CNBC AT LUNCH TIME

The advent of the financial television channel CNBC presented plenty of benefits to the financial community but it also allowed a collection of extrovert practitioners long on theories to voice them in a few minutes of television time. One often sees respectable people making ludicrous (but smart-sounding) statements about properties of the stock market. Among these are statements that blatantly violate the laws of probability. One summer during which I was assiduous at the health club, I often heard such statement as "the real market is only 10% off the highs while the average stock is close to 40% off its highs", which is intended to be indicative of deep troubles or anomalies – some harbinger of bear markets.

There is no incompatibility between the fact that the average stock is down 40% from the highs while the average of all stocks (that is, the market) is down 10% from its own highs. One must consider that the stocks did not all reach their highs *at the same time*. Given that stocks are not 100% correlated, stock A might reach its maximum in January, stock B might reach its maximum in April, but the average of the two stocks A and B might reach its maximum at some time in February. Furthermore, in the event of negatively correlated stocks, if stock A is at its maximum when stock B is at its minimum, then they could both be down 40% from their maximum when the stock market is at its highs! By a law of probability called distribution of the maximum of random variables, the maximum of an average is necessarily less volatile than the average maximum.

YOU SHOULD BE DEAD BY NOW

This brings to mind another common violation of probability by prime-time T.V. financial experts, who may be selected for their looks, charisma and their presentation skills, but certainly not for their incisive minds. For instance, a fallacy that I saw commonly made by a prominent T.V. financial guru goes as follows: "The average American is expected to live 73 years. Therefore if you are 68 you can expect to live five more years, and should plan accordingly". She went into precise prescriptions of how the person should invest for a five more years horizon. Now what if you are 80? Is your life expectancy *minus* seven years? What these journalists confuse is the unconditional and conditional life expectancy. At birth, your unconditional life expectancy may be 73 years. But as you advance in age and do not die, your life expectancy increases along with your life. Why? Because the other people by dying have taken your spot in the statistics, for expectation means average. So if you are 73 and are in good health, you may still have, say, nine years *in expectation*. But the expectation would change, and at 82, you will have another five years, provided of course you are still alive. Even someone 100 years old still has a positive conditional life expectation. Such a statement, when one thinks about it, is not too different from the one that says: *our operation has a mortality rate of 1%. So far we have operated on 99 patients with great success; you are our 100th, hence you have a 100% probability of dying on the table.*

T.V. financial planners may confuse a few people. This is quite harmless. What is far more worrying is the supply of information by non-professionals to professionals; it is to the journalists that we turn next.

THE BLOOMBERG EXPLANATIONS

I have, on my desk, a machine eponymously called a *Bloomberg*^{TM} (after the legendary founder Michael Bloomberg). It acts as a safe e-mail service, a news service, a historical data retrieving tool, a charting system, an invaluable analytical aid and, not least, a screen where I can see the price of securities and currencies. I have gotten so addicted to it that I cannot operate without it, as I would otherwise feel cut off from the rest of the world. I use it to get in contact with my friends, confirm appointments, and solve some of those entertaining quarrels that put some sharpness into life. Somehow, traders who do not have a Bloomberg address do not exist for us (they have to have recourse to the more plebeian internet). But there is one aspect of Bloomberg I would dispense with; the journalist's commentary. Why? Because they engage in explaining things and perpetuate the right-column, left-column confusion in a serious manner. Bloomberg is not the sole perpetrator; it is just that I have not been exposed to newspapers' business sections over the past decade, preferring to read real prose instead.

As I am writing these lines I see the following headlines on my Bloomberg:

→ *Dow is up 1.03 on lower interest rates.*
→ *Dollar down 0.12 yen on higher Japanese surplus.*

and so on for an entire page. If I translate it well, the journalist claims to provide an explanation for something that amounts to *perfect noise*. A move of 1.03 with the Dow at 11,000 constitutes less than a 0.01% move. Such a move does not warrant an explanation. There is nothing there that an honest person can try to explain; there are no reasons to adduce. But like apprentice professors of comparative literature, journalists being paid to provide explanations will gladly and readily provide them. The only solution is for Michael Bloomberg to stop paying his journalists for providing commentary.

Significance: how did I decide that it was perfect noise? Take a simple analogy. If you engage in a mountain bicycle race with a friend across Siberia and, a month later, beat him by one single second, you clearly cannot quite boast that you are faster than him. You might have been helped by something, or it can be just plain randomness, nothing else. That second is not in itself significant enough for someone to draw conclusions. I would not write in my pre-bed-time diary: *cyclist A is better than cyclist B because he is fed with spinach whereas cyclist B has a diet rich in tofu. The reason I am making this inference is because he beat him by 1.3 seconds in a 3,000 mile race.* Should the difference be one week, then I could start analyzing whether tofu is the reason, or if there are other factors.

Causality: there is another problem; even assuming statistical significance, one has to accept a cause and effect, meaning that the event in the market can be linked to the cause proffered. *Post hoc ergo propter hoc* (it is the reason because it came after). Say Hospital A delivered 52% of boys and Hospital B delivered the same year only 48%; would you try to give the explanation that you had a boy *because* it was delivered in hospital A?

Causality can be very complex. It is very difficult to isolate a single cause when there are plenty around. This is called multivariate analysis. For instance, if the stock market can react to U.S. domestic interest rates, the dollar against the yen, the dollar against the European currencies, the European stock markets, the United States balance of payments, United States inflation, and another dozen prime factors, then the journalists need to look at all of these factors, look at their historical effect both in isolation and jointly, look at the stability of such influence, then, after consulting the test statistic isolate the factor if it is possible to do so. Finally, a proper confidence level needs to be given to the factor itself; if it is less that 90% the story would be dead. I can understand why Hume was extremely obsessed with causality and could not accept such inference anywhere.

I have a trick to know if something *real* in the world is taking place. I have set up my Bloomberg monitor to display the price and percentage change of all relevant prices in the world: currencies, stocks, interest rates, and commodities. By dint of looking at the same setup for years, as I keep the currencies in the upper left corner and the various stock markets on the right, I managed to build an instinctive way of knowing if something serious is going on. The trick is to look only at the large percentage changes. Unless something moves by more than its usual daily percentage change, the event is deemed to be noise. Percentage moves are the size of the headlines. In addition, the interpretation is not linear; a 2% move is not twice as significant an event as 1%, it is rather like four times. The headline of the Dow moving by 1.3 points on my screen today has less than one millionth of the significance of the serious 7% drop of October 1997. People might ask me: why do I want everybody to learn some statistics? The answer is that too many people read explanations. We cannot instinctively understand the nonlinear aspect of probability.

FILTERING METHODS

Engineers use methods to clean up the noise from the signal in the data. Did it ever occur to you while talking to your cousin in Australia or the South Pole that the static on the telephone line could be distinguished from the voice of your correspondent? The method is to consider that when a change in amplitude is small, it is more likely to result from noise – with its likelihood of being a signal increasing exponentially as

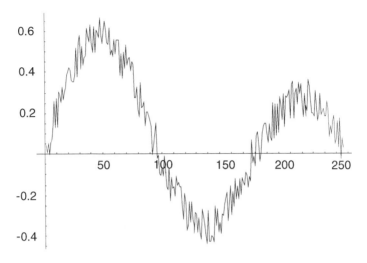

Figure 11.1   Unfiltered Data Containing Signal and Noise.

its magnitude increases. The method is called a smoothing kernel which has been applied in Figures 11.1 and 11.2. But our auditory system is incapable of performing such a function by itself. Likewise our brain cannot see the difference between a significant price change and mere noise, particularly when it is pounded with unsmoothed journalistic noise.

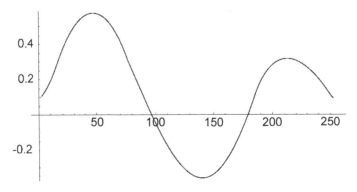

Figure 11.2   Same Data With its Noise Removed.

WE DO NOT UNDERSTAND CONFIDENCE LEVELS

Professionals forget the following reality. It is not the estimate or the forecast that matters so much as the degree of confidence with the opinion. Consider that you are going on a trip one fall morning and need to formulate an idea about the weather conditions prior to packing your luggage. If you expect the temperature to be 60 degrees, plus or minus 10 degrees (say in Arizona), then you would take no snow clothes and no portable electric fan. Now what if you were going to Chicago, where you are told that the weather, while being 60 degrees, will nevertheless vary by about 30 degrees? You would have to pack winter and summer clothes. Here the expectation of the temperature carries little importance concerning the choice of clothing; it is the variance that matters. Your decision to pack is markedly different now that you are told that the variability would be around 30 degrees. Now let us push the point further; what if you were going to a planet where the expectation is also going to be around 60 degrees, but plus or minus 500 degrees? What would you pack?

We can see that my activity in the market depends far less on where I think the market is going so much as it does on the degree of error I allow around such a confidence level.

AN ADMISSION

We close this chapter with the following information: I consider myself as prone to foolishness as anyone I know, in spite of my profession and the time spent building my expertise on the subject. But here is the exception; I know that I am very, very weak on that score. My humanity will try to foil me; I have to stay on my guard. I was born to be fooled by randomness. That will be explored in Part III.

PART III

WAX IN MY EARS -
LIVING WITH RANDOMITIS

O dysseus, the Homerian hero, had the reputation of using guile to overcome stronger opponents. I find the most spectacular use of such guile was against no other opponent than himself.

In book 12 of the *Odyssey*, the hero encounters the sirens, on an island not far from the rocks of Caribde and Scylla. Their songs are known to charm the sailors into madness, causing them to irresistibly cast themselves into the sea off the sirens' coast, and perish. The indescribable beauty of the sirens' songs is contrasted with the moldering corpses of sailors that strayed into the area around them. Odysseus, forewarned by Circe, contrives the following ruse. He fills the ears of all his men with wax, to the point of total deafness, and has himself tied to the mast. The sailors are under strict instructions not to release him. As they approach the sirens' island, the sea is calm and over the water comes the sound of a music so ravishing that Odysseus struggles to get loose, expending an inordinate amount of energy to unrestrain himself. His men tie him even further, until they are safely past the poisoned sounds.

The first lesson I took from the story is not to even attempt to be Odysseus. He is a mythological character and I am not. He can be tied to the mast; I can merely reach the rank of a sailor who needs to have his ears filled with wax.

I AM NOT SO INTELLIGENT

The epiphany I had in my career in randomness came when I understood that I was not intelligent enough, nor strong enough, to even try to fight my emotions. Besides, I believe that I need my emotions to formulate my ideas and get the energy to execute them.

I am just intelligent enough to understand that I have a predisposition to be fooled by randomness – and to accept the fact that I am rather emotional. I am dominated by my emotions – but as an aesthete, I am happy about that fact. I am just like every single character whom I ridiculed in this book. Not only that, but I may be even worse than them because there may be a negative correlation between beliefs and behavior (recall Popper the man). The difference between myself and those I ridicule is that I try to be aware of it. No matter how long I study and try to understand probability, my emotions will respond to a different set of calculations, those that my unintelligent genes want me to handle. If my brain can tell the difference between noise and signal, my heart cannot.

Such unintelligent behavior does not just cover probability and randomness. I do not think I am reasonable enough to avoid getting angry when a discourteous driver blows his horn at me for being one nanosecond late after a traffic light turns green. I am fully aware that such anger is self-destructive and offers no benefit, and that if I were to develop anger for every idiot around me doing something of the sort, I would be long dead. These small daily emotions are not rational. But we need them to function properly. We are designed to respond to hostility with hostility. I have enough enemies to add some spice to my life, but I sometimes wish I had a few more (I rarely go to the movies and need the entertainment). Life would be unbearably bland if we had no enemies on whom to waste efforts and energy.

The good news is that there are tricks. One such trick is to avoid eye contact (through the rear-view mirror) with other persons in such encounters as traffic situations. I try to imagine that the other person is a Martian, rather than a human being. It works sometimes – but it works best when the person presents the appearance of being from a different species. How? I am an avid road cyclist. Recently, as I was riding along with other cyclists, slowing down traffic in a rural area, a small woman in a giant sports utility vehicle opened her window and heaped curses at us. Not only did it not upset me but I did not even interrupt my thoughts to pay attention. When I am on my bicycle, people in large trucks become a variety of dangerous animals, capable of threatening me but incapable of making me angry.

I have, like anyone with strong opinions, a collection of critics among finance academics and economists, annoyed by my attacks on their misuse of probability and unhappy about my branding them as pseudoscientists. I am incapable of taming my emotions when reading their comments. The best I can do is just not read them. Likewise with journalists. Not reading their discussions of markets spares me plenty of emotional expenditure. I will do the same with reviews of this book. Wax in my ears.

The Odyssean Mute Command

Recall that the accomplishment from which I derive the most pride is my weaning myself from television and the news media. I am currently so weaned that it actually costs me more energy to watch television than to perform any other activity, like, say, writing this book. But this did not come without tricks. Without tricks I would not escape the toxicity of the information age. In the trading room of my company I currently have the television set turned on all day with the financial news channel CNBC staging commentator after commentator and CEO after CEO murdering rigor all day long. What is the trick? I have the volume turned completely off. Why? Because when the television set is silent, the babbling person looks ridiculous, exactly the opposite effect as when the sound is on. One sees a person with moving lips and contortions in their facial muscles, taking themselves seriously – but no sound comes out. We are visually but not auditorily intimidated, which causes a dissonance. The speaker's face expresses some excitement, but since no sound comes out, the exact opposite is conveyed. This is the sort of contrast the philosopher Henri Bergson had in mind in his *Treatise on Laughter*, with his famous description of the gap between the seriousness of a gentleman about to walk on a banana skin and the comical aspect of the situation. Television pundits lose their intimidating effect; they even look ridiculous. They seem to be excited about something terribly unimportant. Suddenly pundits become clowns, which is a reason the writer Graham Greene refused to go on television.

I had this idea of stripping people from language while, on a trip, I listened (while brutally jetlagged) to a speech in Cantonese, a language I do not understand, without the benefit of translation. Since I had no possible clue about his subject, the animated orator lost a large share of his dignity. The idea came to me that perhaps I could use a genetic bias, here prejudice, to offset another genetic bias, our predisposition to take information seriously. It seems to work.

This part, the conclusion of this book, presents the human aspect of dealing with uncertainty. I have personally failed in a general insulation from randomness, but I have managed a few tricks.

TWELVE

GAMBLERS' TICKS AND PIGEONS IN A BOX

On gamblers' ticks crowding up my life. Why bad taxi-cab English can help you make money. How I am the fool of all fools, except that I am aware of it. Dealing with my genetic unfitness. No boxes of chocolate under my trading desk.

Taxi-Cab English and Causality

First, a flashback in time to my early days as a trader in New York. Early in my career, I worked at Credit Suisse First Boston, then located in the middle of the block between 52nd and 53rd Street, between Madison and Park Avenue. It was called a Wall Street firm, in spite of its midtown location – I used to claim to work "on Wall Street" in spite of having been lucky enough to set foot only twice in the physical Wall Street, one of the most repulsive areas I have visited east of Newark, New Jersey.

Then, in my twenties, I lived in a book-choked (but otherwise rather bare) apartment in Manhattan's upper east side. The bareness was not ideological; it was simply because I never managed to enter a furniture store, as I would eventually stop at a bookstore along the way and haul bags of books instead. As can be expected, the kitchen was devoid of any form of food and utensils, save for a defective expresso machine, as I learned to cook only very recently (even then ...).

I went to work every morning in a yellow cab, which dropped me off at the corner of Park Avenue and 53rd Street. Cab drivers in New York City are known to be rather untamed and universally unfamiliar with the geography of the place, but, on occasion, one can find a cab driver who can both be unacquainted with the city and skeptic of the universality of the laws of arithmetic. One day I had the misfortune (or perhaps the fortune, as we will see) to ride with a driver who did not seem capable of handling any language known to me, which includes taxi-cab English. I tried to help him navigate south between 74th Street and 53rd Street, but he stubbornly continued the journey an additional block south, forcing me to use the 52nd Street entrance. That day, my trading portfolio made considerable profits, owing to considerable turmoil in currencies; it was then the best day of my young career.

The next day, as usual, I hailed a cab from the corner of 74th Street and Third Avenue. The previous driver was nowhere in sight, perhaps deported back to the old country. Too bad; I was gripped with the unexplainable desire to pay him back for the favor he had done me and surprise him with a gigantic tip. Then I caught myself instructing the new cab driver to take me to the north-east corner of 52nd Street and Park Avenue, exactly where I was dropped off the day before. I was taken aback by my own words ... but it was too late.

When I looked at my reflection in the elevator's mirror, it dawned on me that I wore the exact same tie as the day before – with the coffee stains from the previous day's fracas (my only addiction is to coffee). There was someone in me who visibly believed in a strong causal link between my use of the entrance, my choice of tie and the previous day's market behavior. I was disturbed for acting like a fake, like an actor who impersonated some role that was not his. I felt that I was an impostor. On the one hand, I talked like someone with strong scientific standards, a probabilist focused on his craft. On the other, I had closed superstitions just like one of these blue-collar pit traders. Would I have to go buy a horoscope next?

A little brooding revealed that my life until then had been governed by mild superstitions, me the expert in options and dispassionate calculator of probabilities, a rational trader! It was not the first time that I had acted on mild superstitions of a harmless nature, which I believed were instilled in me by my Eastern Mediterranean roots: one does not grab the salt shaker from the hand of another person risking a falling out; one is to knock on wood upon receiving a compliment; plus many other Levantine beliefs passed on for a few dozen centuries. But like many things that brew and spread around the ancient pond, these beliefs I had taken with a fluctuating mixture of solemnity and mistrust. We consider them more like rituals than truly important actions meant to stave off undesirable turns of the goddess Fortuna – superstitions can instill some poetry in daily life.

The worrying part was that it was the first time that I noticed superstitions creeping into my professional life. My profession is to act like an insurance company, stringently computing the odds based on well defined methods, and making a profit because other people are less rigorous, get blinded by some "analysis", or act with the belief that they are chosen by destiny. But there was too much randomness flooding my occupation.

I detected the rapid accumulation of what is called "gamblers' ticks" surreptitiously developing in my behavior – though minute and barely detectable. Until then these small ticks had escaped me. My mind seemed to be constantly trying to detect a statistical connection between some of my facial expressions and outcome of events. For example, my income started to increase after I discovered my slight near-sightedness and started wearing glasses. Although glasses were not quite necessary, nor even useful, except for night driving, I kept them on my nose as I unconsciously acted as if I believed in the association between performance and glasses. To my brain such statistical association was as spurious as it can get, owing to the reduced sample size, yet this native statistical instinct did not seem to benefit from my expertise in hypothesis testing.

Gamblers are known to develop some behavioral distortions as a result of some pathological association between a betting outcome and some physical move. "Gambler" is about the most derogatory term that could be used in my derivatives profession. As an aside, gambling to me is best defined as an activity where the agent gets a thrill when confronting a random outcome, regardless of whether he has the odds stacked in his favor or against him. Even when the odds are clearly stacked against the gambler, he sometimes transcends the odds by believing that destiny selected him in some manner. This shows in the very sophisticated people one meets in casinos where they normally should not be found. I even ran into world-class probability experts who had a gambling habit on the side, throwing all of their knowledge to the wind. For example, a former colleague of mine and one of the most intelligent people I have ever met, frequently went to Las Vegas, and seemed to be such a turkey that the casino provided him with complimentary luxury suites and transportation. He even consulted a fortune teller prior to taking large trading positions and tried to get reimbursed by our employer.

The Skinner Pigeon Experiment

At 25, I was totally ignorant of the behavioral sciences. I had been fooled by my education and culture into believing that *my superstitions were cultural*, and that, consequently, they could be shed through the exercise of so-called reason. Taken at the general level of society, modern life would eliminate them as science and logic would enter it. But in my case, I was over time getting more sophisticated intellectually, but the floodgates of randomness were bursting and I was becoming more superstitious.

These superstitions needed to be biological – but I was brought up in an era when the dogma was that it was nurture, rarely nature, that was the culprit. Clearly, there was nothing cultural about my link between my wearing glasses and a random market outcome. There was nothing cultural in my link between my use of entrance and my performance as a trader. There was nothing cultural in my wearing the same tie as the day before. Something in us has not developed properly over the past thousand years and I was dealing with the remnant of our old brain.

To probe the point further, we need to look at such formations of causal associations in the lower forms of life. The famous Harvard psychologist B.F. Skinner constructed a box for rats and pigeons, equipped with a switch that the pigeon can operate by pecking. In addition, an electrical mechanism delivers food into the box. Skinner designed the box in order to study more general properties of the behavior of a collection of nonhumans, but it was in 1948 that he had the brilliant idea of ignoring the lever and focusing on the food delivery. He programmed it to deliver food at random to the famished birds.

He saw quite astonishing behavior on the part of the birds; they developed an extremely sophisticated rain-dance type of behavior in response to their ingrained statistical machinery. One bird swung its head rhythmically against a specific corner of the box, others spun their heads anti-clockwise; literally all of the birds developed a specific ritual that progressively became hard-wired into their mind as linked to their feeding.

This problem has a more worrying extension; we are not made to view things as independent from each other. When viewing two events A and B, it is hard not to assume that A causes B, B causes A, or both cause each other. Our bias is immediately to establish a causal link. While to a budding trader this causes hardly any worse costs than a few pennies in cab fare, it can draw the scientist into spurious inference. For it is harder to act as if one were ignorant than as if one were smart; scientists know that it is emotionally harder to reject a hypothesis than to accept it (what is called type I and type II errors) – quite a difficult matter when we have such sayings as *felix qui potuit cognoscere causas* (happy is he who understands what is behind things). It is very hard for us to just shut up. We are not cut out for it. Popper or not, we take things too seriously.

Philostratus Redux

I offered no solution to the problem of statistical inference at a low resolution. I discussed in Chapter 3 the technical difference between noise and meaning – but it is time to discuss the execution. The Greek philosopher Pyrrho, who advocated a life of equanimity and indifference, was criticized for failing to keep his composure during a critical circumstance (he was chased by an ox). His answer was that he found it sometimes difficult to rid himself of his humanity. If Pyrrho cannot stop being human, I do not see why the rest of us should resemble the rational man who acts perfectly under uncertainty as propounded by economic theory. I discovered that much of the rationally obtained results using my computations of the various probabilities do not register deeply enough to impact my own conduct. In other words, I acted like the doctor in Chapter 11 who knew of the 2% probability of the disease, but somehow unwittingly treated the patient as if the ailment had a 95% probability of being there. My brain and my instinct were not acting in concert.

The details are as follows. As a rational trader (all traders boast so) I believe as I discussed before that there is a difference between noise and signal, and that noise needs to be ignored while a signal needs to be taken seriously. I use elementary (but robust) methods that allow me to calculate the expected noise and signal composition of any fluctuation in my trading performance. For example, after registering a profit of $100,000 on a given strategy, I may assign a 2% probability to the hypothesis of the strategy being profitable and 98% probability to the hypothesis that the performance may be the result of mere noise. A gain of $1,000,000, on the other hand, certifies that the strategy is a profitable one, with a 99% probability. A rational person would act accordingly in the selection of strategies, and set his emotions in accordance with his results. Yet I have experienced leaps of joy over results that I knew were mere noise, and bouts of unhappiness over results that did not carry the slightest degree of statistical significance. I cannot help it, but I am emotional and derive most of my energy from my emotions. So the solution does not reside in taming my heart.

Since my heart does not seem to agree with my brain, I need to take serious action to avoid making irrational trading decisions, namely, by denying myself access to my performance report unless it hits a predetermined threshold. This is no different from the divorce between my brain and my appetite when it comes to the consumption of chocolate. I generally deal with it by ascertaining that there are no chocolate boxes under my trading desk.

One of the most irritating conversations I've had is with people who lecture me on *how I should* behave. Most of us know pretty much *how we should* behave. It is the execution that is the problem, not the absence of knowledge. I am tired of the moralizing slow-thinkers who pound me with platitudes like I should floss daily, eat my regular apple and visit the gym outside of the new-year resolution. In the markets the recommendation would be to ignore the noise component in the performance. We need tricks to get us there but before that we need to accept the fact that we are mere animals in need of lower forms of tricks, not lectures.

Finally, I consider myself lucky for not having a cigarette addiction. For the best way to understand how we could be rational in our perception of the risks and probabilities and, at the same time, be foolish while acting on them, would be to have a conversation with a cigarette smoker. For few cigarette smokers remain unaware of the fact that lung cancer strikes one in three of their population. If you remain unconvinced, take a look at the huddling smoking crowd outside the service entrance of the Memorial-Sloan Kettering Cancer Center in New York City's upper East side. You will see dozens of cancer nurses (and, perhaps, doctors) standing outside the entrance with a cigarette in hand as hopeless patients are wheeled in for their treatments.

THIRTEEN

━━┼━━

CARNEADES COMES TO ROME: ON PROBABILITY AND SKEPTICISM

Cato the censor sends Carneades packing. Monsieur de Norpois does not remember his old opinions. Beware the scientist. Marrying ideas. The same Robert Merton helping the author start his firm. Science evolves from funeral to funeral.

A sk your local mathematician to define probability; he would most probably show you how to compute it. As we saw in Chapter 3 on probabilistic introspection, probability is not about the odds, but about the belief in the existence of an alternative outcome, cause, or motive. Recall that mathematics is a tool to meditate, not compute. Again, let us go back to the elders for more guidance – for probabilities were always considered by them as nothing beyond a subjective, and fluid, measure of beliefs.

Carneades Comes to Rome

Around 155 B.C., the Greek post-classical philosopher Carneades of Cyrene came to Rome as one of the three Athenian ambassadors who came to beg the Roman Senate for a political favor. A fine had been levied against the citizens of their city, and they wanted to convince Rome that it was unfair. Carneades represented the Academy, the same argumentative open-air institution where three centuries before Socrates drove his interlocutors to murder him just to get some respite from his arguments. It was now called the New Academy, was no less argumentative, and had the reputation of being the hotbed of skepticism in the ancient world.

On the much anticipated day of his oration, he stood up and delivered a brilliantly argued harangue in praise of justice and how devolving it should be at the top of our motives. The Roman audience was spellbound. It was not just his charisma; the audience was swayed by the strength of the arguments, the eloquence of the thought, the purity of the language, and the energy of the speaker. But that was not the point he wanted to drill.

The next day, Carneades came back, stood up and established the doctrine of uncertainty of knowledge in the most possibly convincing way. How? By proceeding to contradict and refute with no less swaying arguments what he had established so convincingly the day before. He managed to persuade the very same audience and in the same spot that justice should be way down on the list of motivations for human undertakings.

Now the bad news. Cato the elder (the "censor") was among the audience, already quite old, and no more tolerant than he had been during his office of censor. Enraged, he persuaded the Senate to send the three ambassadors packing lest their argumentative spirit muddle the spirit of the youth of the Republic and weaken the military culture. (Cato had banned during his office of censorship all Greek rhetoricians from establishing residence in Rome. He was too much a no-nonsense type of person to accept their introspective expansions.)

Carneades was not the first skeptic in classical times, nor was he the first to teach us the true notion of probability. But this incident remains the most spectacular in its impact on generations of rhetoricians and thinkers. Carneades was not merely a skeptic; he was a dialectician, someone who never committed himself to any of the premises from which he argued, or to any of the conclusions he drew from them. He stood all his life against arrogant dogma and belief in one sole truth. Few credible thinkers rival Carneades in their rigorous skepticism (a class that would include the medieval Arab philosopher Al Gazali, Hume, and Kant – but only Popper came to elevate his skepticism to an all-encompassing scientific methodology). As the skeptics' main teaching was that nothing could be accepted with certainty, conclusions of various degrees of probability could be formed, and these supplied a guide to conduct.

Stepping further back in time and searching for the first known uses of probabilistic thinking in history, we find it harks back to sixth-century (B.C.) Greek Sicily. There, the notion of probability was used in a legal framework by the very first rhetoricians who, when arguing a case, needed to show the existence of a doubt concerning the certainty of the accusation. The first known rhetorician was a Syracusean named Korax who engaged in teaching people how to argue from probability. At the core of his method was the notion of the *most probable*. For example, the ownership of a piece of land, in the absence of further information and physical evidence, should go to the person after whose name it is best known. One of his indirect students, Gorgias, took this method of argumentation to Athens, where it flourished. It is the establishment of such *most probable* notions that taught us to view the possible contingencies as distinct and separable events with probabilities attached to each one of them.

PROBABILITY THE CHILD OF SKEPTICISM

Until the Mediterranean basin was dominated with monotheism, which led to the belief in some form of uniqueness of the truth (to be superceded later by episodes of communism), skepticism had gained currency among many major thinkers – and certainly permeated the world. The Romans did not have a religion *per se*; they were too tolerant to accept a given truth. Theirs were a collection of a variety of flexible and syncretic superstitions. I will not get too theological, except to say that we had to wait for a dozen centuries in the Western world to espouse critical thinking again. Indeed, for some strange reason during the middle ages, Arabs were critical thinkers (through their post-classical philosophical tradition) when Christian thought was dogmatic, then after the renaissance, the roles mysteriously reversed.

One author from antiquity who provides us evidence of such thinking is the garrulous Cicero. He preferred to be guided by probability than allege with certainty – very handy, some said, because it allowed him to contradict himself. This may be a reason for us, who have learned from Popper how to remain self critical, to respect him more, as he did not hew stubbornly to an opinion for the mere fact that he had voiced it in the past. Indeed your average literature professor would fault him for his contradictions and his change of mind.

It was not until modern times that such desire to be free from our own past statements emerged. Nowhere was it made more eloquently than in rioting student graffiti in Paris. The student movement that took place in France in 1968, with the youth no doubt choking under the weight of years of having to sound intelligent and coherent, produced, among other jewels, the following demand:

We demand the right to contradict ourselves!

Monsieur de Norpois's Opinions

Modern times provide us with a depressing story. Self-contradiction is made culturally to be shameful, a matter that can prove disastrous in science. Marcel Proust's novel *In Search of Time Lost* features a semi-retired diplomat, Marquis de Norpois, who, like all diplomats before the advent of the fax machine, was a socialite who spent considerable time in salons. The narrator of the novel sees Monsieur de Norpois openly contradicting himself on some issue (some prewar rapproche-ment between France and Germany). When reminded of his previous position, Monsieur de Norpois did not seem to recall it. Proust reviles him:

Monsieur de Norpois was not lying. He had just forgotten. One forgets rather quickly what one has not thought about with depth, what has been dictated to you by imitation, by the passions surrounding you. These change, and with them so do your memories. Even more than diplomats, politicians do not remember opinions they had at some point in their lives and their fibbings are more attributable to an excess of ambition than a lack of memory.

Monsieur de Norpois is made to be ashamed of the fact that he expressed a different opinion. Proust did not consider that the diplomat might have changed his mind. We are supposed to be faithful to our opinions. One becomes a traitor otherwise.

Now I hold that Monsieur de Norpois should be a trader. One of the best traders I have ever encountered in my life, Nigel Babbage, has the remarkable attribute of being completely free of any path dependence in his beliefs. He exhibits absolutely no embarrassment buying a given currency on a pure impulse, when only hours ago he might have voiced a strong opinion as to its future weakness. What changed his mind? He does not feel obligated to explain it.

The public person most visibly endowed with such a trait is George Soros. One of his strengths is that he revises his opinion rather rapidly, without the slightest embarrassment. The following anecdote illustrates Soros's ability to reverse his opinion in a flash. The French playboy trader Jean-Manuel Rozan discusses the following episode in his autobiography[12] (disguised as a novel in order to avoid legal bills). The protagonist (Rozan) used to play tennis in the Hamptons on Long Island with Georgi Saulos, an "older man with a funny accent", and sometimes engage in discussions about the market, not initially knowing how important and influential Saulos truly was. One week-end, Saulos exhibited in his discussion a large amount of bearishness, with a complicated series of arguments that the narrator could not follow. He was obviously short the market. A few days later, the market rallied violently, making record highs. The protagonist worried about Saulos, asked him at their subsequent tennis encounter if he was hurt. "We made a killing", Saulos said. "I changed my mind. We covered and went very long".

It was this very trait that, a few years later, affected Rozan negatively and almost cost him a career. Soros gave Rozan in the late 1980s 20 million dollars to speculate with (a sizeable amount at the time), which allowed him to start a trading company (I was almost dragged into it). A few days later, as Soros was visiting Paris, they discussed markets over lunch. Rozan saw Soros becoming distant. He then completely pulled the money, offering no explanation. What characterizes real speculators like Soros from the rest is that their activities are devoid of path dependence. They are totally free from their past actions. Every day is a clean slate.

PATH DEPENDENCE OF BELIEFS

There is a simple test to define path dependence of beliefs. Say you own a painting you bought for $20,000, and owing to rosy conditions in the art market, it is now worth $40,000. If you owned no painting, would you still acquire it at the current price? If you would not, then you are said to be married to your position. There is no rational reason to keep a painting you would not buy at its current market rate – only an emotional investment. Many people get married to their ideas all the way to the grave. Beliefs are said to be path dependent if the sequence of ideas is such that the first one dominates.

There are reasons to believe that, for evolutionary purposes, we may be programmed to build a loyalty to ideas in which we have invested time. Think about the consequences of being a good trader outside of the market activity, and deciding every morning at 8 a.m. whether to keep the spouse or if it is not better to part with him or her for a better emotional investment elsewhere. Or think of a politician who is so rational that, during a campaign, he changes his mind on a given matter because of fresh evidence and abruptly switches political parties. That would make rational investors who evaluate trades in a proper way a genetic oddity – perhaps a rare mutation. Some medical researchers find that purely rational behavior on the part of humans is a sign of a defect in the amygdala, that the subject is, literally, a psychopath. Could Soros have a genetic flaw that makes him rational as a decision maker?

Such trait of absence of marriage to ideas is indeed rare among humans. Just as we do with children, we support those in whom we have a heavy investment of food and time until they are able to propagate our genes, so we do with ideas. An academic who became famous for espousing an opinion is not going to voice anything that can possibly devalue his own past work and kill years of investment. People who switch parties become traitors, renegades, or, worst of all, apostates (those who abandoned their religion were punishable by death).

Computing Instead of Thinking

There is another story of probability other than the one I introduced with Carneades and Cicero. Probability entered mathematics with gambling theory, and stayed there as a mere computational device. Recently, an entire industry of "risk measurers" emerged, specializing in the application of these probability methods to assess risks in the social sciences. Clearly, the odds in games where the rules are clearly and explicitly defined are computable and the risks consequently measured. But not in the real world. For mother nature did not endow us with clear rules. The game is not a deck of cards (we do not even know how many colors there are). But somehow people "measure" risks, particularly if they are paid for it. I have already discussed Hume's problem of induction and the occurrence of black swans. Here I introduce the scientific perpetrators.

Recall that I have waged a war against the charlatanism of some prominent financial economists for a long time. The points are as follows. One Harry Markowitz received something called the Nobel Memorial Prize in Economics (which in fact is not even a Nobel Prize as it is granted by the Swedish central bank in honor of Alfred Nobel – it was never in the will of the famous man). What is his achievement? By creating an elaborate method of computing *future* risk if one knows *future* uncertainty; in other words if markets had clearly defined rules – which is clearly not the case. Now I explained the point to a cab driver who laughed at the fact that someone ever thought that there was any scientific method to understand markets and predict their attributes. Somehow when one gets involved in financial economics, owing to the culture of the field, one becomes likely to forget these basic facts.

An immediate result of Dr. Markowitz's theory was the near collapse of the financial system in the summer of 1998 (as we saw in Chapters 1 and 5) by Long Term Capital Management ("LTCM"), a Greenwich, Connecticut fund that had for principals two of Dr. Markowitz's colleagues, "Nobel" as well. They are Drs. Robert Merton (the one in Chapter 3 trouncing Shiller) and Myron Scholes. Somehow they thought they could scientifically "measure" their risks. They made absolutely no allowance in the LTCM episode for the possibility of their not understanding markets and their methods being wrong. That was not a hypothesis to be considered. I happen to specialize in profiting from the black swans and the breakdown of the system, and make bets against financial economists. Suddenly I started getting some irritating fawning respect, along with paychecks from the market. Drs. Merton and Scholes helped put your humble author on the map and caused the birth of your humble crisis-hunter's firm, Empirica – as capital started flowing to people who did the exact opposite of what they did for a living.

One would think that when scientists make a mistake, they develop a new science that incorporates what has been learned from it. When academics blow up trading, one would expect them to integrate such information in their theories and make some heroic statement to the effect that they were wrong, but that now they have learned something about the real world. Nothing of the sort. Instead they complain about the behavior of their counterparts in the market who pounced on them like vultures, thus exacerbating their downfall. Accepting what has happened, clearly the courageous thing to do, would invalidate the ideas they have built throughout an entire academic career. All of the principals who engaged in a discussion of the events partook of a masquerade of science by adducing *ad hoc* explanations and putting the blame on a rare event (problem of induction: how did they know it was a rare event?). They spent their energy defending themselves rather than trying to make a buck with what they learned. Again compare them with Soros who walks around telling whomever has the patience to listen to him that he is fallible. My lesson from Soros is to start every meeting at my trading boutique by convincing everyone that we are a bunch of idiots who know nothing and are mistake prone, but happen to be endowed with the rare privilege of knowing it.

From Funeral to Funeral

I conclude with the following saddening remark about scientists in the soft sciences. People confuse science and scientists. Science is great, but individual scientists are dangerous. They are human; they are marred by the biases humans have. Perhaps even more. For most scientists are hard headed, otherwise they would not derive the patience and energy to perform the Herculean tasks asked of them, like spending 18 hours a day perfecting their doctoral thesis.

A scientist may be forced to act like a cheap defense lawyer rather than a pure seeker of the truth. A doctoral thesis is "defended" by the applicant; it would be a rare situation to see the student change his mind upon being supplied with a convincing argument. But science is better than scientists. It was said that science evolves from funeral to funeral. After the LTCM collapse, a new financial economist will emerge, who will integrate such knowledge in his science. He will be resisted by the older ones but, again, they will be much closer to their funeral date than he.

FOURTEEN

BACCHUS ABANDONS ANTONY

*Montherlant's death. Stoicism is not the stiff upper lip, but the
illusion of victory of man against randomness. It is so easy to be
heroic. Randomness and personal elegance.*

When the classicist aristocratic French writer Henry de Montherlant was told that he was about to lose his eyesight to a
degenerative disease, he found it most appropriate to take his own life.
Such is the end that becomes a classicist. Why? Because the stoic's
prescription was precisely to elect what one can do to control one's
destiny in front of a random outcome. At the end, one is allowed to
choose between no life at all and what one is given by destiny; we
always have an option against uncertainty. But such an attitude is not
limited to stoics; both competing sects in the ancient world, stoicism and
Epicurianism recommended such control (the difference between the
two resides in minor technicalities – neither philosophies meant then
what is commonly accepted today in middlebrow culture).

Being a hero does not necessarily mean such an extreme act as
getting killed in battle or taking one's life – the latter is only recommended in a narrow set of circumstances and considered cowardly
otherwise. Having control over randomness can be expressed in the
manner one acts in the small and the large. Recall that epic heroes

were judged by their actions, not by the results. No matter how sophisticated our choices, how good we are at dominating the odds, randomness will have the last word. We are left only with dignity as a solution – dignity defined as the execution of a protocol of behavior that does not depend on the immediate circumstance. It may not be the optimal one, but it certainly is the one that makes us feel best. *Grace under pressure*, for example. Or in deciding not to toady up to someone, whatever the reward. Or in fighting a duel to save face. Or in signaling to a prospective mate during courtship: "listen, I have a crush on you; I am obsessed with you, but I will not do a thing to compromise my dignity. Accordingly, the slightest snub and you will never see me again".

This last chapter will discuss randomness from a totally new angle; philosophical but not the *hard* philosophy of science and epistemology as we saw in Part I with the *black swan problem*. It is a more archaic, *softer* type of philosophy, the various guidelines that the ancients had concerning the manner a man of virtue and dignity deals with randomness – there was no real *religion* at the time (in the modern sense). It is worthy of note that before the spread of what can be best called Mediterranean monotheism, the ancients did not believe enough in their prayers to influence the course of destiny. Their world was dangerous, fraught with invasions and reversals of fortune. They needed substantial prescriptions in dealing with randomness. It is such beliefs that we will outline next.

Notes on Jackie O.'s Funeral

If a stoic were to visit us, he would feel represented by the following poem. To many (sophisticated) lovers of poetry, one of the greatest poets who ever breathed is C.P. Cavafy. Cavafy was an Alexandrian Greek civil servant with a Turkish or Arabic last name who wrote almost a century ago in a combination of classical and modern Greek a lean poetry that seems to have eluded the last fifteen centuries of Western literature. Greeks treasure him like their national monument.

Most of his poems take place in Syria (his Grecosyrian poems initially drew me to him), Asia Minor, and Alexandria. Many people believe it worth learning formal semi-classical Greek just to savor his poems. Somehow their acute aestheticism stripped of sentimentality provides a relief from centuries of mawkishness in poetry and drama. He provides a classical relief for those of us who were subjected to the middle-class valued melodrama as represented by Dickens's novels, romantic poetry, and Verdi's operas.

I was surprised to hear that Maurice Tempelsman, last consort of Jackie Kennedy Onassis, read Cavafy's valedictory *Apoleipein o Theos Antonion* (The God Abandons Antony) at her funeral. The poem addresses Marc Antony, who has just lost the battle against Octavius and was forsaken by Bacchus the god who until then had protected him. It is one of the most elevating poems I have ever read, beautiful because it was the epitome of such dignified aestheticism – and because of the gentle but edifying tone of the voice of the narrator advising a man who had just received a crushing reversal of fortune.

The poem addresses Antony, now defeated and betrayed (according to legend, even his horse deserted him to go to his enemy Octavius). It asks him to just bid her farewell, Alexandria the city that is leaving him. It tells him not to mourn his luck, not to enter denial, not to believe that his ears and eyes are deceiving him. Antony, do not degrade yourself with empty hopes. Antony,

> *Just listen while shaken by emotion but not with the coward's imploration and complaints.*

While shaken with emotion. No stiff upper lip. There is nothing wrong and undignified with emotions – we are cut to have them. What is wrong is not following the heroic, or at least, the dignified path. That is what *stoicism* truly means. It is the attempt by man to get even with probability. I need not be nasty at all and break the spell of the poem and its message, but I cannot resist some cynicism. A couple of decades later, Cavafy, while dying of throat cancer did not quite follow the prescription. Deprived of his voice by the surgeons, he used to randomly enter undignified spells of crying and cling to his visitors, preventing them from leaving his death room.

Some history. I said that stoicism has rather little to do with the stiff upper lip notion that we believe it means. Started as an intellectual movement in antiquity by a Phoenician Cypriot, Zeno of Kitium, it developed by Roman time into a life based on a system of virtues – in the ancient sense when virtue meant *virtu*, the sort of belief in which virtue is its own reward. There developed a social model for a stoic person, like the gentlemen in Victorian England. Its tenets can thus be summarized as follows: the stoic is a person who combines the qualities of wisdom, upright dealing, and courage. The stoic will thus be immune from life's gyrations as he will be superior to the wounds from some of life's dirty tricks. But things can be carried to the extreme; the stern Cato found it beneath him to have human feelings. A more human version can be read in Seneca's *Letters From a Stoic*, a soothing and surprisingly readable book that I distribute to my trader friends (Seneca also took his own life when cornered by destiny).

Randomness and Personal Elegance

The reader knows my opinion on unsolicited advice and sermons on how to behave in life. Recall that ideas do not truly sink in when emotions come into play; we do not use our rational brain outside of classrooms. Self-help books (even when they are not written by charlatans) are largely ineffectual. Good, enlightened (and "friendly") advice and eloquent sermons do not register for more than a few moments when they go against our wiring. The interesting thing about stoicism is that it plays on dignity and personal aesthetics, which are part of our genes. Start stressing personal elegance at your next misfortune. Exhibit *sapere vivere* ("know how to live") in all circumstances.

Dress at your best on your execution day (shave carefully); try to leave a good impression on the death squad by standing erect and proud. Try not to play victim when diagnosed with cancer (hide it from others and only share the information with the doctor – it will avert the platitudes and nobody will treat you like a victim worthy of their pity; in addition the dignified attitude will make both defeat and victory feel equally heroic). Be extremely courteous to your assistant when you lose money (instead of taking it out on him as many of the traders whom I scorn routinely do). Try not to blame others for your fate, even if they deserve blame. Never exhibit any self pity, even if your significant other bolts with the handsome ski instructor or the younger aspiring model. Do not complain. If you suffer from a benign version of the "attitude problem", like my childhood friend Camille Abousleiman, do not start playing nice guy if your business dries up (he sent a heroic e-mail to his colleagues informing them "less business, but same attitude"). The only article Lady Fortuna has no control over is your behavior. Good luck.

EPILOGUE: SOLON TOLD YOU SO

—+—

BEWARE THE LONDON TRAFFIC JAMS

A couple of years after we left him looking at John smoking a cigarette with a modicum of *schadenfreude*, Nero's skepticism ended up paying off. Simultaneously as he beat the 28% odds, up to the point of complete cure, he made a series of exhilarating personal and professional victories. Not only did he end up sampling the next level of wealth but he got the riches right when other Wall Street hot shots got poor, which could have allowed him to buy the goods they owned at very large discounts, if he wanted to. But he acquired very little, and certainly none of the goods Wall Streeters usually buy. But Nero did engage in occasional excess.

Friday afternoon traffic in London can be dreadful. Nero started spending more time there. He developed an obsession with traffic jams. One day he spent five hours moving West from his office in the City of London towards a cottage in the Cotswolds where he stayed most weekends. The frustration prompted Nero to get a helicopter flying license, through a crash course in Cambridgeshire. He realized that the train was probably an easier solution to get out of town for the weekend, but he felt the urge for a pet extravagance. The other result of his frustration was his no less dangerous commuting on a bicycle between his flat in Kensington and his office in the City.

Nero's excessive probability consciousness in his profession somehow did not register fully into his treatment of physical risk. For Nero's helicopter crashed as he was landing it near Battersea Park on a windy day. He was alone in it. In the end the black swan got its man.

NOTES

1. This is the Dryden translation of Plutarch's *Lives*.
2. For an example of pseudoscientific historicism, I suggest Francis Fukuyama, 1992, *The End of History and the Last Man*, New York: Free Press.
3. Richard Dawkins, 1990 (1970), *The Selfish Gene*, 2nd ed., Oxford: Oxford University Press.
4. Alan Sokal, 1996, Transgressing the Boundaries: Toward a Transformative Hermeneutics of Quantum Gravity, *Social Text* (spring–summer).
5. www.monash.edu.au
6. Brian Magee, 1997, *Confessions of a Philosopher*, London: Weidenfeld & Nicolson.
7. Malachi Haim Hacohen, 2001, *Karl Popper, The Formative Years, 1902–1945: Politics and Philosophy in Interwar Vienna*, New York: Cambridge University Press.
8. R. Sullivan, A. Timmerman and H. White, 1999, Data-Snooping, Technical Trading Rule Performance and the Bookstrap, *Journal of Finance*, October.
9. I thank my correspondent Francesco Corielli from Bocconi for his remark on meta-analysis.
10. Deborah J. Bennett, 1998, *Randomness*, Cambridge, MA: Harvard University Press.
11. Antonio Damasio, 1995, *Descartes' Error: Emotion, Reason, and the Human Brain*, New York: Avon Books. See also Joseph Ledoux, 1998, *The Emotional Brain: The Mysterious Underpinning of Emotional Life*, New York: Touchstone Books.
12. Jean-Manuel Rozan, 1999, *Le fric*, Paris: Michel Lafon.

INDEX

✛

About TEXERE

TEXERE seeks to become the most progressive and authoritative voice in business publishing by cultivating and enhancing ideas that will illuminate the global business landscape. Our name defines the spirit of our vision: TEXERE is the ancient Latin verb 'to weave.' In an increasingly global business community, we seek to create an intersection where authors and readers can share the best thinking and the latest ideas. We want to leverage the expertise and insights of leading thinkers by weaving them with TEXERE's capability to deliver them to the marketplace.

To learn more and become a part of our community visit us at:

www.etexere.com

and

www.etexere.co.uk

About the Typeface

This book was set in $10\frac{1}{2}/14$ Sabon. This elegant typeface is a descendant of the types of Claude Garamond and was designed by Jan Tschichold in 1964. The roman design is based on a Garamond specimen printed by Konrad F. Berner, who was married to the widow of another printer Jacques Sabon. The italic design is based on types by Robert Granjon, a contemporary of Garamond's.